SCHOLAST

MW01157210

Success With

Reading Tests

New York • Toronto • London • Auckland • Sydney
Mexico City • New Delhi • Hong Kong • Buenos Aires

Teaching *Resources*

The *Scholastic Success With Reading Tests* series is designed to help you help students succeed on standardized tests. In this workbook for fifth grade, the 15 four-page tests are culled from the reading skills practice tests provided three times a year to *Scholastic News Senior Edition* subscribers, with some new and revised material. By familiarizing children with the skills, language, and formats they will encounter on state and national tests, these practice tests will boost confidence and help raise scores.

The questions supporting each test are specifically designed to review the following skills:

- Finding the Main Idea
- Reading for Detail
- Understanding Vocabulary
- Making Inferences
- Sequencing
- Understanding Cause and Effect
- Understanding Author's Purpose
- Understanding Fact and Opinion

Note that the tests in the second half of the book are slightly more difficult. These are designed to be given later in the school year.

In addition to helping children prepare for "real" tests, the practice tests in this workbook may be used as a diagnostic tool, to help you detect individual students' strengths and weaknesses, or as an instructional tool, for oral reading and discussion.

Keep in mind that our practice tests are just that—practice. These tests are not standardized. They should not be used to determine grade level, to compare one student's performance with that of others, or to evaluate teachers' abilities.

HOW TO ADMINISTER THE TESTS:

Before administering each test, you may wish to review with students some basic test-taking strategies, such as reading the questions before reading the passages.

- Establish a relaxed atmosphere. Explain to students that they will not be graded and that they are taking the test to practice for "real" tests down the road.
- Review the directions, then read the samples in each section and discuss the answers. Be sure to pay close attention to the directions in the vocabulary or study skills section on the last page of each test.
- To mimic the atmosphere of a real test, you may wish to set time limits. Students should be able to complete the reading comprehension section (the first three pages of each test) in 20 to 25 minutes. Allow an additional 10 minutes for the vocabulary or study skills portion on the last page of each test.
- Use the **Answer Key** provided on pages 63–64 to check students' work; or if desired, have students check their own answers.

State Standards Correlations

To find out how this book helps you meet your state's standards, log on to **www.scholastic.com/ssw**

Cover design by Ka-Yeon Kim-Li

ISBN 978-0-545-20109-4

20 21 22   131   20 19

Reading Skills Practice Test I

READING COMPREHENSION

Read each story. Then fill in the circle that best completes each sentence or answers each question.

Have you ever seen someone on the beach with a sunburn? A sunburn can be quite painful. If the burn is really bad, the skin might blister and peel. Sunburn is caused by the sun's powerful ultraviolet (UV) rays. Wearing sunscreen can **shield** your skin from those damaging rays.

I. What is the main idea of this story?
   ○ **A.** Ultraviolet rays cause sunburn.
   ○ **B.** Sunburn can cause fever.
   ○ **C.** Sunscreen makes skin peel.
   ○ **D.** It gets hot at the beach.

2. In this story, the word **shield** means
   ○ **A.** burn
   ○ **B.** lift.
   ○ **C.** protect.
   ○ **D.** open.

A.	For thousands of years, the Inuit people have lived in what is now the northwest part of Canada. For the last 150 years, the Canadian government has ruled the land. In 1999, the government agreed to let the Inuit **govern** part of Canada's Northwest Territory.

Since April 1, 1999, the Canadian map has included the land of Nunavut, which means "our land" in Inuktitut, the Inuit language. The Inuit wanted control of this land because it is the land of their ancestors.

I. In this story, the word **govern** means
   ○ **A.** build.
   ○ **B.** map.
   ○ **C.** rule.
   ○ **D.** live.

2. You can guess from the story that
   ○ **A.** Canada's government once took over Inuit land.
   ○ **B.** Canada's government is unfair.
   ○ **C.** the Inuit cannot speak English.
   ○ **D.** many Canadian people will soon be homeless.

3. Which would come first on a time line?
   ○ **A.** The Inuit make a deal with Canada's government.
   ○ **B.** The Canadian government begins ruling the Inuit's land.
   ○ **C.** The Inuit settle in Canada.
   ○ **D.** Nunavut appears on a map.

B. Animals depend on plants and other animals for food. The relationship among these animals and plants is called a food chain. The food chain keeps nature in balance. Here's how it works:

1. Producers: Plants and other organisms that provide food for animals make up the first link in a food chain.
2. Herbivores: These are animals that eat only plants. Called "prey," they are hunted by meat eaters.
3. Carnivores: These meat eaters feed on herbivores. They are also called "predators." When they die, their remains fertilize the ground and help plants grow.

I. What is the best title for this story?
- ○ **A.** "Plant-Eating Animals"
- ○ **B.** "Understanding the Food Chain"
- ○ **C.** "Predators"
- ○ **D.** "Plants That Need Animals"

2. Animals that eat meat are called
- ○ **A.** herbivores.
- ○ **B.** producers.
- ○ **C.** prey.
- ○ **D.** carnivores

3. You can guess from this story that
- ○ **A.** herbivores are hungrier that carnivores.
- ○ **B.** herbivores are small animals.
- ○ **C.** carnivores eat lots of vegetables.
- ○ **D.** each link in the food chain is important.

C. In Greek mythology, Zeus and Hera were the leaders of the Greek gods. They were husband and wife. Hera sometimes became angry with Zeus when he spent too much time away from home.

Sometimes, Zeus went to the mountains to play with the forest creatures who lived there. Hera always chased after him because she thought Zeus was wasting time. But every time Hera entered the forest, a charming creature named Echo chatted with her and distracted her until Zeus had escaped.

When Hera figured out Echo had been tricking her, she was **furious**. "Your talk has made a fool of me!" she screamed. "From now on you will have nothing to say, except what others say to you first!"

From that day on, poor Echo could only repeat the last word of what others said.

I. This story is mostly about
- ○ **A.** Greek gods.
- ○ **B.** Greece.
- ○ **C.** forests.
- ○ **D.** tricks.

2. You can guess from the story that
- ○ **A.** Zeus was tall and handsome.
- ○ **B.** Echo lost her voice.
- ○ **C.** Hera was very gentle.
- ○ **D.** Echo lived in the forest.

3. In this story, the word **furious** means
- ○ **A.** angry.
- ○ **B.** happy.
- ○ **C.** foolish.
- ○ **D.** tricky.

4. Zeus and Hera were
- ○ **A.** soldiers.
- ○ **B.** forest creatures.
- ○ **C.** married.
- ○ **D.** human.

D. When you play a sport, do you feel that you must win—or else? The Youth Sports Institute in Michigan surveyed 26,000 boys and girls on this topic, and found that many feel pushed to be the best.

Where does the pressure come from? Some kids put pressure on themselves, but many say that parents and coaches are also to blame.

They say these adults care only about the final score—not whether kids tried hard or had a good time.

I. What is the main idea of this article?
- ○ **A.** Fewer kids should play baseball.
- ○ **B.** Youth sports are always fun.
- ○ **C.** Many kids feel a lot of pressure to win at sports.
- ○ **D.** Parents should be banned from going to kids' games.

2. Which of the statements is a *fact*?
- ○ **A.** Sports pressure is the worst part of kids' sports.
- ○ **B.** The Youth Sports Institute surveyed 26,000 kids.
- ○ **C.** Winning is important.
- ○ **D.** Coaches should not be allowed to pressure players.

3. The author wrote this article to
- ○ **A.** tell why baseball is good exercise.
- ○ **B.** tell kids to quit playing sports.
- ○ **C.** tell about the history of youth sports.
- ○ **D.** tell about a problem in youth sports.

4. The article probably goes on to talk about
- ○ **A.** solving the problem of sports pressure.
- ○ **B.** baseball training camps for kids.
- ○ **C.** ways for teams to win more games.
- ○ **D.** youth football programs.

E. In 1844, young Elizabeth Blackwell dreamed of becoming a doctor. There was just one problem: No medical school in the U.S. would accept a woman as a student. Blackwell convinced several doctors to teach her privately. Then, in 1847, she was accepted by a small college in New York. She graduated at the top of her class.

Blackwell traveled to Paris, France, where she studied at a hospital. Even after losing her sight in one eye, Blackwell did not give up her work as a doctor. In the 1850s, she returned to the U.S. and **established** a hospital for women and children. Today, we remember Elizabeth Blackwell as the trailblazer who opened the field of medicine for women in America.

I. In this story, the word **established** means
- ○ **A.** set up.
- ○ **C.** named.
- ○ **B.** cured.
- ○ **D.** lost.

2. What is the best title for this story?
- ○ **A.** "Elizabeth Blackwell: Opening College Doors"
- ○ **B.** "Elizabeth Blackwell: First Woman Doctor"
- ○ **C.** "The Autobiography of Elizabeth Blackwell"
- ○ **D.** "Famous Doctors in History"

3. Which of these is an *opinion*?
- ○ **A.** Blackwell lost sight in one eye.
- ○ **B.** Blackwell became a doctor.
- ○ **C.** Blackwell lived in the 1800s.
- ○ **D.** Blackwell was very brave.

4. You can guess from this story that Elizabeth Blackwell
- ○ **A.** got good grades in college.
- ○ **B.** had French parents.
- ○ **C.** eventually became totally blind.
- ○ **D.** died in 1860.

VOCABULARY
Which Word Is Missing?

In each of the following paragraphs, a words is missing. First, read each paragraph. Then choose the missing word from the list beneath the paragraph. Fill in the circle next to the word that is missing.

Sample:

The car suddenly stopped in the middle of the road. It had run out of _____ The driver had forgotten to fill up the gas tank.

- ○ **A.** miles
- ○ **B.** fuel
- ○ **C.** water
- ○ **D.** popcorn

I. Some really large animals live on the plains of Africa. You might think the biggest ones would be the mightiest hunters, but that's not the case at all. Some of the world's biggest animals eat nothing but leaves, grasses, and shrubs. Instead of hunting other animals, these huge creatures _____ on plant life to survive.

- ○ **A.** dwell
- ○ **B.** sit
- ○ **C.** grow
- ○ **D.** graze

2. The largest plant eater of all is the African Elephant. In fact, the African elephant is the largest land _____ in the entire world! An adult elephant can weigh as much as 12,000 pounds. And a baby elephant is not exactly tiny: It can weigh up to 250 pounds at birth!

- ○ **A.** shark
- ○ **B.** soil
- ○ **C.** mammal
- ○ **D.** farmer

3. Another very large African plant eater is the white rhinoceros. It is second in size only to the elephant. The adult white rhino can weigh up to 5,000 pounds, or two-and-a-half _____

- ○ **A.** pounds
- ○ **B.** tons
- ○ **C.** ounces
- ○ **D.** feet

4. The black rhino is a _____ of the white rhino. Although the two are kin, the black rhino doesn't get nearly as large. At 3,000 pounds, though, the adult black rhino is still pretty big. Both rhinos are very good at using their horns to break off tree branches for dinner.

- ○ **A.** relative
- ○ **B.** neighbor
- ○ **C.** friend
- ○ **D.** killer

5. A somewhat smaller African plant eater is the hippopotamus. At 700 pounds, the adult hippo seems almost _____ compared with an elephant or a rhino —but you'd still feel pretty small standing next to one! A hippo has teeth about 20 inches long. They are excellent tools for munching coarse plants.

- ○ **A.** giant
- ○ **B.** desperate
- ○ **C.** dainty
- ○ **D.** loyal

6. The hippo's teeth also come in handy for fighting off crocodiles. That's important, because hippos spend lots of time in rivers, where crocs live. Hippos have sensitive skin that can easily get too dry. They hang out in the river to keep their skin _____

- ○ **A.** nasty
- ○ **B.** moist
- ○ **C.** brown
- ○ **D.** clean

Reading Skills Practice Test 2

READING COMPREHENSION

Read each story. Then fill in the circle that best completes each sentence or answers each question.

To turn 16 dogs to the right, yell, "Come gee!" To turn them to the left, say, "Come haw!" You'll need to know that to enter the Iditarod, the world's longest dogsled race. During the Iditarod, your dogs will have to pull you and your sled over 1,000 miles of frozen ground, from Anchorage to Nome, Alaska.

1. The Iditarod is
   ○ A. a command to turn dogs to the right.
   ○ B. a type of sled.
   ○ C. the world's longest dogsled race.
   ○ D. a route from Nome to Anchorage, Alaska.

2. From this story, you can conclude that the Iditarod is
   ○ A. easy.
   ○ B. difficult.
   ○ C. something anyone can do.
   ○ D. hated outside of Alaska.

A. Although he held an important research job, Billy Jo the chimpanzee was headed for life in a warehouse, with no friends and nothing to do. Then two Canadians gave him and 14 other chimps in similar situations a home on their farm. They felt that Billy Jo and his friends deserved a nice retirement home.

That's because these chimps were part of a research project at New York University to find cures for AIDS and hepatitis. Life at the lab was painful and lonely. The chimps had many operations, tests, and shots. One chimp had 137 liver operations. Another was tranquilized, or knocked out with drugs, 279 times.

1. Why did Billy Jo deserve a nice retirement home?
   ○ A. He wore purple boxer shorts.
   ○ B. He withstood painful research.
   ○ C. He was 30 years old.
   ○ D. He had lots of friends.

2. What is the best title for this story?
   ○ A. "How We Find Cures For Diseases"
   ○ B. "Chimps Retire to Life on the Farm"
   ○ C. "Research Projects at New York University"
   ○ D. "AIDS and Hepatitis: Two Deadly Diseases"

3. The next paragraph might talk about
   ○ A. other animals used in tests.
   ○ B. life in New York City.
   ○ C. how Billy Jo and his friends do on the farm.
   ○ D. cures for AIDS and Hepatitis

B.   Say *adios* to holes in your teeth. Scientists at Guy's Hospital in London, England, have designed a vaccine that stops cavities in their tracks. And best of all, you won't need a shot.

Cavities form when bacteria cling to tooth surfaces and turn sugars from food into a type of acid. The acid eats away at a tooth's outer layer, known as the enamel, and leaves a hole. But dentists plan to paint your teeth with a tasteless, colorless vaccine that fights tooth decay.

Believe it or not, the most important ingredient in the vaccine comes from tobacco plants. This ingredient prevents the bacteria that causes most tooth decay from sticking to teeth. So pretty soon, having your mouth painted once a year could keep you cavity-free for life!

I.   What happens after sugars from food are turned into acid?
  ○ **A.** The acid eats away at the tooth's outer layer.
  ○ **B.** Dentists paint the tooth with a vaccine.
  ○ **C.** The acid turns into an ingredient found in tobacco plants.
  ○ **D.** The acid plugs already existing holes in the tooth.

2.   Which is an *opinion*?
  ○ **A.** Scientists have developed an anti-cavity vaccine.
  ○ **B.** Acid from food sugar causes tooth decay.
  ○ **C.** The important ingredient in the vaccine comes from tobacco plants.
  ○ **D.** The best thing about the vaccine is not having to get shots.

3.   The tooth's outer layer is also called the
  ○ **A.** enamel.   ○ **C.** bacteria.
  ○ **B.** vaccine.   ○ **D.** plaque.

C.   The falcons were dying. The pollution in the air was making the shells of their eggs too thin. When nesting mothers sat on the eggs, they would break. If something wasn't done, the fastest-winged animal in the world would die-off forever.

All across America, animals were dying. Gray wolves, brown pelicans, bald eagles, and others were all in danger of becoming extinct. So 25 years ago, the American government took action. The Endangered Species Act was signed into law.

This law gave a branch of the government called the Fish and Wildlife Service the power to save endangered plants or animals. Any animal on the list would be protected by law from hunters or pollution. It was an experiment that had never been tried before. No one knew if it would work.

But it did work! In recent years, several animals and plants have been considered for de-listing. That means that they could be taken off the endangered-species list, and they are no longer considered in danger of becoming extinct.

I.   What happens to animals on the endangered-species list?
  ○ **A.** They are protected by law from hunters and pollution.
  ○ **B.** They are kept in zoos until they reproduce.
  ○ **C.** They begin dying off.
  ○ **D.** They get taken off after a year.

2.   Why were the falcons dying?
  ○ **A.** They were being over-hunted.
  ○ **B.** Pollution was making the shells of their eggs too thin.
  ○ **C.** Gray wolves were eating them.
  ○ **D.** They had been on the endangered-species list for 25 years.

D. Are you an average American kid? If so, you probably watch TV for almost 5 hours a day. That means you spend more than two months a year glued to the tube. But some kids are just saying, "No," to TV.

Take Meghan Kelley of Pembroke, Massachusetts. She used to spend a lot of her free time in front of the TV. But in 1996, Meghan kicked her TV habit for good. Her days of tuning in ended when she and her classmates at North Pembroke Elementary School took part in National TV-Turnoff Week.

After the first week, Meghan decided to test herself further. "I wanted to see how long I could go without TV," Meghan said. "Could I do it for a year?" The answer turned out to be **affirmative**!

Although sometimes she missed

TV, Meghan found life without cartoons and commercials more interesting. She joined two soccer leagues and began playing basketball and softball. Because Meghan was studying more, she also got much better grades.

I. The main purpose of this story is to
○ **A.** sell TVs.   ○ **C.** scare.
○ **B.** amuse.   ○ **D.** inform.

2. In this story, the word **affirmative** means
○ **A.** no.   ○ **C.** maybe.
○ **B.** yes.   ○ **D.** sort of.

3. After she stopped watching TV, Meghan
○ **A.** made better grades.
○ **B.** lost all her friends.
○ **C.** couldn't play sports.
○ **D.** missed TV so much she became depressed.

E. Wanda and Tina had been best friends for years. They did everything together. That's why Wanda was so surprised one day when Tina wouldn't talk to her. She had saved Tina a seat in the lunchroom, but when Tina came in she went off and sat by herself.

Wanda didn't know what was wrong. Could Tina be mad at her? She thought about what she had done and said recently. Was Tina upset because Wanda had done better on the history test than her? No, Tina didn't care about that kind of thing. She was happy that Wanda did well in school.

Wanda decided to find out what was the matter. She walked over to where Tina was sitting. "Tina," she said softly, "Is something wrong?"

Tina looked up, momentarily **perplexed**. Then she realized who it was. "Oh, hi, Wanda," she said. "Yes, something is wrong. My cat Zorro died today. I've been really sad. Thanks for asking. You're a true friend." Then she smiled. Wanda sat down next to her friend and gave her a big hug.

I. In this story the word **perplexed** means
○ **A.** happy.   ○ **C.** bored.
○ **B.** intelligent.   ○ **D.** confused.

2. Why was Tina ignoring Wanda?
○ **A.** She was sad that her cat had died.
○ **B.** She was mad that Wanda had done well on the history test.
○ **C.** She didn't want to be Wanda's friend anymore.
○ **D.** She wanted to eat lunch by herself.

3. From the story, you might guess that
○ **A.** Tina doesn't like Wanda.
○ **B.** Wanda doesn't like Tina.
○ **C.** Tina and Wanda are in the same history class.
○ **D.** Tina and Wanda are sisters.

4. What is the best title for this story?
○ **A.** "A True Friend"
○ **B.** "Lunchroom Laughs"
○ **C.** "Not a Friend"
○ **D.** "When a Pet Dies

VOCABULARY

Synonyms

Read the underlined word in each phrase. Mark the word below it that has the same (or close to the same) meaning.

Sample:

wool and cotton <u>blend</u>
- ○ **A.** fabric
- ○ **B.** material
- ○ **C.** mix
- ○ **D.** layer

1. I <u>resemble</u> him
   - ○ **A.** look like
   - ○ **B.** resent
   - ○ **C.** hate
   - ○ **D.** watch

2. a big <u>guffaw</u>
   - ○ **A.** scream
   - ○ **B.** yell
   - ○ **C.** laugh
   - ○ **D.** cry

3. <u>devour</u> the food
   - ○ **A.** throw out
   - ○ **B.** eat
   - ○ **C.** cook
   - ○ **D.** feed

4. <u>possess</u> a book
   - ○ **A.** own
   - ○ **B.** lend
   - ○ **C.** carry
   - ○ **D.** read

5. a great <u>location</u>
   - ○ **A.** job
   - ○ **B.** place
   - ○ **C.** scene
   - ○ **D.** train

6. <u>capable</u> hands
   - ○ **A.** able
   - ○ **B.** unable
   - ○ **C.** clumsy
   - ○ **D.** fast

7. looking for <u>insight</u>
   - ○ **A.** contentment
   - ○ **B.** understanding
   - ○ **C.** courtesy
   - ○ **D.** forgiveness

Antonyms

Read the underlined word in each phrase. Mark the word below it that means the opposite or nearly the opposite.

Sample:

I <u>adore</u> her
- ○ **A.** love
- ○ **B.** hate
- ○ **C.** like
- ○ **D.** dislike

1. a <u>wintry</u> day
   - ○ **A.** cold
   - ○ **B.** warm
   - ○ **C.** long
   - ○ **D.** tiring

2. <u>smug</u> look
   - ○ **A.** happy
   - ○ **B.** unsure
   - ○ **C.** sad
   - ○ **D.** pleased

3. <u>embrace</u> an idea
   - ○ **A.** support
   - ○ **B.** learn
   - ○ **C.** dislike
   - ○ **D.** reject

4. <u>overjoyed</u> expression
   - ○ **A.** unhappy
   - ○ **B.** beaming
   - ○ **C.** reserved
   - ○ **D.** guarded

5. <u>classic</u> movie
   - ○ **A.** long
   - ○ **B.** old
   - ○ **C.** short
   - ○ **D.** new

6. <u>considerable</u> amount
   - ○ **A.** strange
   - ○ **B.** expensive
   - ○ **C.** small
   - ○ **D.** large

7. beg to <u>differ</u>
   - ○ **A.** digest
   - ○ **B.** defer
   - ○ **C.** agree
   - ○ **D.** assume

Reading Skills Practice Test 3

READING COMPREHENSION

Read each story. Then fill in the circle that best completes each sentence or answers each question.

SAMPLE

How cool can glasses get? Try these on. New experimental glasses plug into the brain and help blind people "see" again. A tiny video camera and a distance-measuring machine sit on the lenses. The camera takes a picture and sends the image into a computer worn on a belt. The computer hooks up to the brain through wires and sends signals to the part of the brain that controls sight.

I. What is the best title for this story?
- ○ **A.** "The Power of Cameras"
- ○ **B.** "Helping People See"
- ○ **C.** "Cameras and Computers"
- ○ **D.** "Being Blind"

A. What do you think of when you hear the word "anaconda"? If you're like many people, you think of a giant, man-eating snake that lives in the Amazon. But you would be wrong.

Although anacondas do live in the Amazon region of South America, they do not eat humans. They do eat animals as large as deer, however. An anaconda kills its prey by giving it a deadly squeeze. This **lethal** hug cuts off the victim's air supply and blood flow.

Scientists still need to find out more about these powerful snakes. For instance, no one really knows how they reproduce.

I. How does an anaconda kill its prey?
- ○ **A.** by squeezing it
- ○ **B.** by biting it
- ○ **C.** by drowning it
- ○ **D.** by eating it

2. In this story, the word **lethal** means
- ○ **A.** friendly.
- ○ **B.** painful.
- ○ **C.** tight.
- ○ **D.** deadly.

3. The purpose of this article is to
- ○ **A.** persuade you that anacondas are beautiful.
- ○ **B.** inform you about anacondas in general.
- ○ **C.** warn you that anacondas are dangerous.
- ○ **D.** amaze you with the size of anacondas.

B.   Shelley Langdon couldn't wait for summer vacation to start. This year her family was going to rent a beach house on the Outer Banks in North Carolina. Shelley had always heard that these barrier islands were beautiful, but she'd never been there.

   To get to their beach house, the Langdons drove for hours. Finally, they crossed a bridge over the sound. When Shelley's dad came off the bridge and made a right, Shelley was amazed. She could see water on both sides of her. On one side, the sound was blue and sparkling, full of boats. On the other, waves crashed against golden sand.

   The Langdon's house, like all the others near it, was up on stilts. A wooden walkway led down from the deck to the beach. Shelley hurriedly pulled on her bathing suit and ran down to the water. There, she was in for a surprise! Out beyond the breakers were two porpoises, leaping and frolicking in the waves!

I.   Based on this story, which of the following statements might be true?
   ○ **A.** North Carolina is not a coastal state.
   ○ **B.** Shelley was very excited about her beach vacation.
   ○ **C.** Shelley's parents don't like the beach very much.
   ○ **D.** The Langdons live very near the Outer Banks.

2.   Why was Shelley surprised?
   ○ **A.** The beach house was on stilts.
   ○ **B.** There were porpoises playing in the waves.
   ○ **C.** It was a long drive to get to the beach.
   ○ **D.** The Outer Banks were very ugly.

3.   What amazed Shelley during the drive?
   ○ **A.** The fact that she could see water on both sides.
   ○ **B.** The fact that her parents fought all the time.
   ○ **C.** The fact that North Carolina had Outer Banks.
   ○ **D.** The fact that their house was not right on the beach.

C.   These days almost everyone knows that olive oil is good for you. But what most people may not realize is that olive oil is used for a lot more than just food. People make soap out of it, polish diamonds with it, and burn it for light. In ancient times, boiling olive oil was even used as a weapon of war.

   Traditionally, olive oil was mainly used by people in Mediterranean countries. But these days, more and more people all over the world are discovering that olive oil may be the best oil for cooking. In the United States, people use five times more olive oil today than they did 20 years ago.

   Ninety-nine percent of the world's olive oil is still produced in Mediterranean countries. Spain leads the list in producing the most olive oil, followed by Italy, Greece, and Turkey.

I.   Which of these is an *opinion*?
   ○ **A.** Olive oil is used for a lot more than just food.
   ○ **B.** Olive oil may be the best oil for cooking.
   ○ **C.** Americans use five times more olive oil than they did 20 years ago.
   ○ **D.** Ninety-nine percent of the world's olive oil is produced in Mediterranean countries.

2.   The biggest producer of olive oil is
   ○ **A.** Italy.
   ○ **B.** Turkey.
   ○ **C.** Greece.
   ○ **D.** Spain.

3.   You can conclude from this article that
   ○ **A.** people in the Mediterranean region only use olive oil.
   ○ **B.** Americans don't like olive oil very much.
   ○ **C.** olive oil is very versatile.
   ○ **D.** olive oil is an important crop for countries in Asia.

D. Can you imagine being trapped on a ship for nine months? That's what happened to an expedition led by Sir Ernest Shackleton.

Shackleton and his crew were trying to reach Antarctica when their ship, the *Endurance*, became trapped in polar ice on January 18, 1915. For nine months they waited for the ice to break up. Finally, in October, the crew abandoned the ship and set sail in three rickety lifeboats.

Hundreds of miles later, the men reached **barren** Elephant Island. Shackleton realized that they could not survive there. So, he and five other men set out in one of the lifeboats for an 800-mile journey to South Georgia Island. They knew that there were people there who could help them.

Seventeen days later, the men arrived. Shackleton took a ship back to Elephant Island and rescued the rest of his crew. Amazingly, everyone was still alive. After over a year of cold, frostbite, and starvation, the men from the *Endurance* were safe at last.

1. What happened after Shackleton arrived at South Georgia Island?
- ○ **A.** He rescued the rest of his crew.
- ○ **B.** He set sail in a lifeboat.
- ○ **C.** The *Endurance* got trapped in the ice.
- ○ **D.** The crew waited nine months for the ice to break up.

2. In this story, the word **barren** means
- ○ **A.** large.
- ○ **C.** mountainous.
- ○ **B.** lifeless.
- ○ **D.** forested.

3. Why did Shackleton and five men set sail from Elephant Island in a lifeboat?
- ○ **A.** They wanted to reach Antarctica.
- ○ **B.** Their ship was trapped in ice.
- ○ **C.** They wanted to see friends on South Georgia Island.
- ○ **D.** They knew the crew could not survive on Elephant Island.

E. Hunger is not just a problem for the poor countries of the world. Even in the United States, there are plenty of people who don't get enough to eat. Some of these people are children. In 2014, there were nearly 16 million kids in the United States whose families sometimes didn't have enough food.

Hunger can have much more serious **consequences** than just a growling stomach. Children dealing with hunger pains have trouble paying attention in school. They don't have the energy to run around on the playground during recess. And not getting enough to eat for a long time can slow a kid's growth and brain development.

What can you do to help stop hunger? Giving time to programs that feed hungry children is a good place to start. Try volunteering at a soup kitchen in your community. Here's what one volunteer had to say about helping to feed hungry kids in his hometown: "It makes me really happy to see the kids eat. All kids have the right to eat."

1. In this article, the word **consequences** means
- ○ **A.** effects.
- ○ **C.** illnesses.
- ○ **B.** problems.
- ○ **D.** losses.

2. According to the story, which of the following is *not* a consequence of hunger?
- ○ **A.** a lack of energy
- ○ **B.** bad skin
- ○ **C.** slow growth
- ○ **D.** trouble paying attention

3. From this story you can conclude that
- ○ **A.** hunger is not a problem among children in the U.S.
- ○ **B.** there is nothing we can do to help fight hunger.
- ○ **C.** kids who grow up hungry may develop serious problems.
- ○ **D.** you don't need to eat to learn.

VOCABULARY

Synonyms

Read the underlined word in each phrase. Mark the word below it that has the same (or close to the same) meaning.

Sample:

quite <u>reluctant</u>
- ○ **A.** eager
- ○ **B.** unwilling
- ○ **C.** unhappy
- ○ **D.** surprised

1. <u>bestow</u> this
   - ○ **A.** give
   - ○ **B.** take
   - ○ **C.** tow
   - ○ **D.** allow

2. with <u>liberty</u>
   - ○ **A.** triumph
   - ○ **B.** faith
   - ○ **C.** freedom
   - ○ **D.** caution

3. very <u>evident</u>
   - ○ **A.** unlikely
   - ○ **B.** obvious
   - ○ **C.** wise
   - ○ **D.** unclear

4. <u>gape</u> at
   - ○ **A.** sneer
   - ○ **B.** squint
   - ○ **C.** smile
   - ○ **D.** stare

5. <u>minor</u> problems
   - ○ **A.** small
   - ○ **B.** large
   - ○ **C.** difficult
   - ○ **D.** easy

6. <u>swivel</u> around
   - ○ **A.** look
   - ○ **B.** turn
   - ○ **C.** fly
   - ○ **D.** float

7. <u>contribute</u> aid
   - ○ **A.** purchase
   - ○ **B.** donate
   - ○ **C.** return
   - ○ **D.** accept

Antonyms

Read the underlined word in each phrase. Mark the word below it that means the opposite or nearly the opposite.

Sample:

<u>idle</u> worker
- ○ **A.** hard
- ○ **B.** lazy
- ○ **C.** busy
- ○ **D.** retired

1. feel <u>panic</u>
   - ○ **A.** calm
   - ○ **B.** upset
   - ○ **C.** disgust
   - ○ **D.** content

2. <u>spectacular</u> event
   - ○ **A.** amazing
   - ○ **B.** joyful
   - ○ **C.** tragic
   - ○ **D.** ordinary

3. <u>smug</u> expression
   - ○ **A.** delighted
   - ○ **B.** self-satisfied
   - ○ **C.** calm
   - ○ **D.** unsure

4. <u>wary</u> glance
   - ○ **A.** carefree
   - ○ **B.** cautious
   - ○ **C.** timid
   - ○ **D.** quick

5. <u>inferior</u> brand
   - ○ **A.** exterior
   - ○ **B.** popular
   - ○ **C.** superior
   - ○ **D.** expensive

6. <u>carefree</u> attitude
   - ○ **A.** unbelievable
   - ○ **B.** laughing
   - ○ **C.** happy
   - ○ **D.** serious

7. <u>clammy</u> grip
   - ○ **A.** cold
   - ○ **B.** firm
   - ○ **C.** icy and wet
   - ○ **D.** warm and dry

Copyright © Scholastic Inc.

Reading Skills Practice Test 4

READING COMPREHENSION

Read each story. Then fill in the circle that best completes each sentence or answers each question.

Everyone knows that spinach is good for you. But who knew that it was first used as a treat for cats? That's right, cats. Spinach was originally grown in ancient Persia. The ancient Persians used it to satisfy the finicky appetites of their cats. Soon people began to love it, too. Today, people all over the world cook with this versatile vegetable.

1. What is the best title for this story?
○ **A.** "Green Vegetables"
○ **B.** "Persian Cats"
○ **C.** "Versatile Vegetables"
○ **D.** "Spinach"

2. Why was spinach originally grown?
○ **A.** because people loved it
○ **B.** because cats loved it
○ **C.** because it's healthy
○ **D.** because it's versatile

A. You're standing by the locker and hear two kids yelling. Their voices get louder and louder. You just know a fight is going to break out. How do you stop it?

If you're a peer mediator, you know how to handle the problem. Peer mediators are students who are trained to help solve arguments before they turn into fights.

When a disagreement breaks out, two peer mediators step in. They listen to both sides and ask both kids how they want to see the problem **resolved**. If both kids agree to the terms, the mediators draw up a contract that each kid signs.

As long as the kids stick to the agreement, everyone wins. Many schools have had less fighting and fewer suspensions since they started using peer mediation.

1. What are peer mediators?
○ **A.** teachers who have been trained to stop fights
○ **B.** students who have been trained to solve arguments
○ **C.** students who fight a lot
○ **D.** students who get suspended a lot

2. In this story, the word **resolved** means
○ **A.** worked out.   ○ **C.** ignored.
○ **B.** reported.   ○ **D.** forgotten about.

3. The purpose of this story is to
○ **A.** persuade you that peer mediators don't work.
○ **B.** inform you about peer mediators.
○ **C.** warn you that fighting is a problem in schools.
○ **D.** amuse you with school-fight stories.

B. You may already know that the Taj Mahal is in India. You may know that many people consider it one of the world's most beautiful buildings. But did you know that this marble masterpiece was built for love?

Emperor Shah Jahan built the Taj Mahal to honor his wife, Mumtaz Mahal. She died in 1629. They had been married for 17 years. The emperor was heartbroken. He decided to honor her with a monument.

The Taj Mahal took more than 20 years to build. Twenty-thousand people worked on it. Experts were brought in from as far away as Europe. The building was finally finished in 1653. It quickly became famous. For more than 300 years, people have flocked to see this stunning monument to love.

I. Which of these is an *opinion*?
- ○ **A.** Twenty-thousand people worked on the Taj Mahal.
- ○ **B.** The building was finished in 1653.
- ○ **C.** The Taj Mahal is the most beautiful building in the world.
- ○ **D.** Shah Jahan was heartbroken when his wife, Mumtaz Mahal, died.

2. How long were Shah Jahan and Mumtaz Mahal married?
- ○ **A.** 12 years
- ○ **B.** 17 years
- ○ **C.** 20 years
- ○ **D.** 30 years

3. What is a good title for this story?
- ○ **A.** "Great Buildings of the World"
- ○ **B.** "Built for Love"
- ○ **C.** "Indian Emperors"
- ○ **D.** "Mumtaz Mahal"

C. There are four things you need to know about Malik Jones. 1. He's in my homeroom. 2. He plays baseball. 3. He gets good grades. 4. He's the most annoying person who ever lived.

I mean, why would a person always stare at me, or talk about my hair, unless it was to annoy me? No matter where I am, Malik is sure to walk by and make some comment. Everyone else thinks it's funny. I just think it's annoying.

So the other day, I finally confronted him. "Malik Jones," I said, "What makes you think you can always talk about my hair?" He looked startled for a minute. "Well," he finally said, "I like your hair. That's why I'm always talking about it. I think it's beautiful." Did I mention that Malik Jones is one of the nicest guys who ever lived?

I. Which of these is an *opinion*?
- ○ **A.** Malik plays baseball.
- ○ **B.** Malik gets good grades.
- ○ **C.** Malik is in the speaker's homeroom.
- ○ **D.** Malik is the most annoying person who ever lived.

2. How would you describe the speaker?
- ○ **A.** shy   ○ **C.** quiet
- ○ **B.** opinionated   ○ **D.** boring

3. You can conclude from this story's ending that
- ○ **A.** the speaker still finds Malik annoying.
- ○ **B.** the speaker likes Malik now.
- ○ **C.** Malik doesn't like the speaker.
- ○ **D.** Malik and the speaker are related.

D. Eighteen-year-old Billy Campbell was riding harder than he had ever ridden before. His horse was **exhausted**. Its chest and sides were foaming with sweat. Campbell hated to push the horse any faster. But he just had to make it to the next station.

Billy Campbell was a rider on the Pony Express. The Pony Express was the nation's first "express" mail delivery service. It was set up in 1860 to carry mail from Missouri to California.

The Pony Express riders were all young men like Billy Campbell. They had to be light of weight and excellent horsemen. Each rider galloped at least 75 miles a day, changing horses several times.

The Pony Express was a success. It got mail to California faster than ever before. Unfortunately, it was also short-lived. A new coast-to-coast telegraph system soon made the Pony Express unnecessary. It was shut down a year and a half after it began.

I. Why did the Pony Express go out of business?
  ○ **A.** The telegraph replaced it.
  ○ **B.** It was too dangerous.
  ○ **C.** It ran out of horses.
  ○ **D.** It wasn't a success.

2. In this story, the word **exhausted** means
  ○ **A.** lively.   ○ **C.** very tired.
  ○ **B.** very fast.   ○ **D.** alert.

3. The Pony Express carried mail from
  ○ **A.** Ohio to Texas.
  ○ **B.** Colorado to Oregon.
  ○ **C.** Boston to Cleveland.
  ○ **D.** Missouri to California.

4. What is the best title for this story?
  ○ **A.** "The History of the Telegraph"
  ○ **B.** "Riding Horses"
  ○ **C.** "The Story of Billy Campbell"
  ○ **D.** "The Pony Express"

E. Endangered animals are big business among some pet sellers. It's illegal to import or sell endangered animals in the United States. But some people try to smuggle them in just the same. Here are a few outrageous endangered animal smuggling stories.

• Guess what officials in Sweden found inside a woman's blouse? Live baby grass snakes—65 of them! The woman planned to start a reptile farm. Instead, she was arrested for smuggling!

• Imagine someone bringing a sackful of endangered tortoises onboard a plane—as carry-on luggage. The luggage was labeled "coconuts." This trick worked until the "coconuts" started to crawl inside the bag!

• One smuggler wore a very valuable piece of clothing. A padded vest hid 40 eggs of Australia's endangered black palm cockatoo—one of the smartest parrots on

Earth. The eggs were worth at least $10,000 each. That's a $400,000 vest!

I. In this article, the word illegal means
  ○ **A.** against the law. ○ **C.** fear.
  ○ **B.** dangerous.   ○ **D.** wonderful.

2. What animal did one smuggler claim were coconuts?
  ○ **A.** snakes   ○ **C.** tortoises
  ○ **B.** parrots   ○ **D.** cockatoos

3. The main purpose of this story is to
  ○ **A.** persuade you that smuggling is bad.
  ○ **B.** inform you that people train endangered animals.
  ○ **C.** entertain you with funny stories about smuggling animals.
  ○ **D.** instruct you on how to catch smugglers.

VOCABULARY

Synonyms

Read the underlined word in each phrase. Mark the word below it that has the same (or close to the same) meaning.

Sample:

comic situation
- ○ **A.** sad
- ○ **B.** formal
- ○ **C.** tense
- ○ **D.** funny

1. gape at
   - ○ **A.** scream
   - ○ **B.** stare
   - ○ **C.** point
   - ○ **D.** laugh

2. a weird feeling
   - ○ **A.** bad
   - ○ **B.** good
   - ○ **C.** strange
   - ○ **D.** happy

3. a throng of people
   - ○ **A.** crowd
   - ○ **B.** line
   - ○ **C.** wall
   - ○ **D.** scattering

4. a funny notion
   - ○ **A.** joke
   - ○ **B.** face
   - ○ **C.** idea
   - ○ **D.** game

5. forthright talk
   - ○ **A.** loud
   - ○ **B.** scared
   - ○ **C.** smooth
   - ○ **D.** straight

6. murky water
   - ○ **A.** clear
   - ○ **B.** rough
   - ○ **C.** muddy
   - ○ **D.** deep

7. luxurious furnishings
   - ○ **A.** uncomfortable
   - ○ **B.** attractive
   - ○ **C.** expensive
   - ○ **D.** cheap

Antonyms

Read the underlined word in each phrase. Mark the word below it that means the opposite or nearly the opposite.

Sample:

damp room
- ○ **A.** wet
- ○ **B.** dry
- ○ **C.** large
- ○ **D.** tiny

1. noisy party
   - ○ **A.** quiet
   - ○ **B.** loud
   - ○ **C.** crowded
   - ○ **D.** empty

2. reckless behavior
   - ○ **A.** careless
   - ○ **B.** careful
   - ○ **C.** proud
   - ○ **D.** humble

3. reject the answer
   - ○ **A.** turn down
   - ○ **B.** withhold
   - ○ **C.** shout
   - ○ **D.** accept

4. coarse crumbs
   - ○ **A.** cake
   - ○ **B.** bread
   - ○ **C.** fine
   - ○ **D.** chunky

5. scaly skin
   - ○ **A.** smooth
   - ○ **B.** dry
   - ○ **C.** dark
   - ○ **D.** light

6. distinguished visitor
   - ○ **A.** important
   - ○ **B.** unimportant
   - ○ **C.** pretentious
   - ○ **D.** disliked

7. offensive odor
   - ○ **A.** nasty
   - ○ **B.** strong
   - ○ **C.** pleasing
   - ○ **D.** sweet

Reading Skills Practice Test 5

READING COMPREHENSION

Read each story. Then fill in the circle that best completes each sentence or answers each question.

Do you like animals? If so, think about veterinary medicine as a **profession**. Veterinarians treat all animals, not just pets. Many vets specialize in treating farm animals. Others work at zoos. Still others try to prevent the spread of diseases from animals to humans. To become a vet, you must attend college and veterinary school.

1. In this story the word **profession** means
   - ○ **A.** hospital.
   - ○ **B.** job.
   - ○ **C.** school.
   - ○ **D.** hobby.

2. This story is mostly about
   - ○ **A.** vet school.
   - ○ **B.** diseases.
   - ○ **C.** veterinarians.
   - ○ **D.** farm animals.

A. In 1787, 55 delegates from 12 states gathered in Philadelphia to write the U.S. Constitution. Future President George Washington led the convention. Other famous attendees included James Madison, Benjamin Franklin, and Alexander Hamilton.

At that time, the U.S. was governed by the Articles of Confederation. This document had been adopted in 1781. The delegates did not think the Articles of Confederation set up a strong central government. They wanted to create a new law of the land. It took the delegates 16 weeks to **draft** our Constitution. It went into effect in 1789, after it was ratified by the states.

1. The Articles of Confederation functioned as the nation's governing document
   - ○ **A.** until 1781.
   - ○ **B.** after 1789.
   - ○ **C.** for just 16 weeks.
   - ○ **D.** before the Constitution was adopted.

2. In this story, the word **draft** means
   - ○ **A.** write.
   - ○ **B.** discard.
   - ○ **C.** abolish.
   - ○ **D.** call to war.

3. You can guess that
   - ○ **A.** most Constitution writers later became Presidents.
   - ○ **B.** the U.S. Constitution is long.
   - ○ **C.** the Constitution gives some power to a central government.
   - ○ **D.** some states refused to ratify the Constitution.

B. Some American deserts have become battlegrounds for fights between dune-buggy drivers and environmentalists. Many drivers like to race their buggies across deserts. They enjoy the open spaces, sandy surface, and challenging dunes. But environmentalists argue that buggies can hurt unique desert animals. For example, the desert tortoise in California's Mojave Desert is an endangered species. Dune buggies have killed many tortoises and destroyed their homes in the sand.

1. Environmentalists would probably like
   ○ **A.** to ban buggies from the desert.
   ○ **B.** to outlaw buggies everywhere.
   ○ **C.** to move to the Mojave Desert.
   ○ **D.** to drive dune buggies.

2. The story would probably go on to talk about
   ○ **A.** endangered birds.
   ○ **B.** other endangered desert animals.
   ○ **C.** unique animals at the zoo.
   ○ **D.** tortoises as pets.

3. The author wrote this story to
   ○ **A.** inform.   ○ **C.** entertain.
   ○ **B.** persuade.   ○ **D.** inspire.

C. In 1995, an ancient mummy was found on Mount Ampato in Peru. Buried 500 years ago, the body had been preserved by freezing temperatures. Its burial site was **exposed** when a volcano melted the mountain's snowcap.

Experts say the body belonged to an Inca girl. The Incas ruled much of South America for over a hundred years. Found with the mummy were several Inca artifacts. Experts are studying them to learn more about the Incas.

1. What is the best title for this story?
   ○ **A.** "All About Mummies"
   ○ **B.** "An Inca Mummy"
   ○ **C.** "Who Were the Incas?"
   ○ **D.** "Peruvian Artifacts"

2. In this story, the word **exposed** means
   ○ **A.** destroyed.   ○ **C.** frozen.
   ○ **B.** opened.   ○ **D.** uncovered.

D. Bike helmets are made of hard foam that absorbs the force of a fall. But if a helmet does not fit, it will not protect the head properly. To make sure your helmet has the right fit, follow these steps:
   • Try on helmets. A helmet shouldn't be too tight, but it shouldn't be so big that it **jostles** back and forth.
   • Stick soft adhesive pads on the inside of the helmet to make it fit just right.
   • Keep the front of your helmet just above your eyebrows when you ride.
   • Make sure the chin strap fits securely under your chin.

1. What is the best title for this story?
   ○ **A.** "Helmets: Get the Perfect Fit"
   ○ **B.** "Biking: Rules of the Road"
   ○ **C.** "Buying a Bike"
   ○ **D.** "Bike Helmet Laws"

2. In this story, the word **jostles** means
   ○ **A.** teases.   ○ **C.** rides.
   ○ **B.** sticks.   ○ **D.** moves.

3. This story is best for someone who
   ○ **A.** rides on busy streets.
   ○ **B.** has a new helmet.
   ○ **C.** is buying a new helmet.
   ○ **D.** rides a mountain bike.

E. Albert Einstein was born in Germany in 1879. As a child, Einstein was slow in school. Some teachers thought he wasn't very bright.

Einstein did not get discouraged. He grew up to develop ideas about time and energy that changed science forever. One of his theories explained the way light beams travel. That discovery made TV possible!

In 1933, Einstein fled from religious persecution in Nazi Germany and came to America. Here, he worked on atomic energy with other scientists. Although the atom bomb helped the U.S. end World War II, Einstein was always against using atomic energy to harm people. After the war, he worked for international peace.

I. Which of these is an *opinion* about Einstein?
○ **A.** He wasn't very bright.
○ **B.** He was born in Germany.
○ **C.** He studied light beams.
○ **D.** He moved to America.

2. Which of these events occurred last?
○ **A.** Einstein went to school.
○ **B.** The atom bomb was created.
○ **C.** Einstein fled Germany.
○ **D.** World War II ended.

3. Einstein fled Germany because
○ **A.** of World War II.
○ **B.** his theories were controversial.
○ **C.** of religious persecution.
○ **D.** he couldn't find work.

F. Dear Travel Section Editor,

Last week's story on Yellowstone and Yosemite national parks was terrific. I would like to make a suggestion for a future article. How about a story on smaller, less well-known parks and monuments? I can suggest three.

The Craters of the Moon National Monument in Idaho contains some of the country's strangest scenery. Its lava flows, volcanic cones, and ice caves will astound visitors. Another of my favorite parks is Indiana Dunes National Lakeshore. You might not expect big sand dunes in Indiana, but there they are! Visitors can swim, hike, and climb at Lake Michigan's shore. Finally, for an educational trip, there's Women's Rights National Historical Park. Located in Seneca Falls, New York, it contains the site of the first Women's Rights Convention. Visitors learn about the struggle of women to achieve voting rights.

Sincerely,
A National Park Fan

I. The letter's main idea is that
○ **A.** some smaller national parks are interesting.
○ **B.** tourists like parks.
○ **C.** the travel section is boring.
○ **D.** parks have strange scenery.

2. Seneca Falls is the site of
○ **A.** Yosemite.
○ **B.** Yellowstone.
○ **C.** Craters of the Moon.
○ **D.** Women's Rights Park.

3. The editor has already run a story on
○ **A.** Craters of the Moon.
○ **B.** Yosemite.
○ **C.** Idaho.
○ **D.** Indiana Dunes.

4. You can guess that
○ **A.** last week's article was about Craters of the Moon.
○ **B.** the writer has seen Yosemite.
○ **C.** the writer lives in Idaho.
○ **D.** Yellowstone is more well-known than Indiana Dunes.

STUDY SKILLS
Reading a Line Graph

Study this line graph about immigration to the U.S. Then choose the best answer for each question.

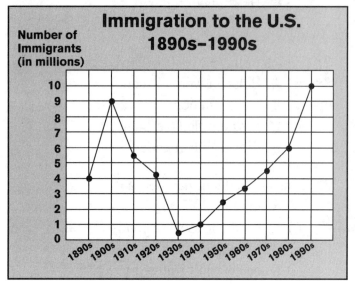

**Immigration to the U.S.
1890s–1990s**

Number of Immigrants (in millions)

I. This line graph shows immigration
○ **A.** before 1870.
○ **B.** to Europe.
○ **C.** from the 1890s to 1990s.
○ **D.** from Europe and Asia only.

2. The fewest immigrants arrived in the
○ **A.** 1930s. ○ **C.** 1940s.
○ **B.** 1900s. ○ **D.** 1950s.

3. About how many immigrants arrived in the U.S. in the 1980s?
○ **A.** 6 thousand ○ **C.** 5.5 million
○ **B.** 6 million ○ **D.** 4.5 million

4. What can you tell about the 1920s?
○ **A.** There were fewer than 3 million immigrants.
○ **B.** Immigration reached its peak.
○ **C.** Most immigrants were Asian.
○ **D.** There were just over 4 million immigrants.

Reading an Index
**Study this section of an index from a book about U.S. history.
Then choose the best answer for each question.**

Index
immigration to the U.S., 33–74:
Ellis Island, 33–40
from Africa, 55–61
from Asia, 41–44, graph, 42
from Europe, 45–50, illus. 47
from South America, 51–54
in the 1990s, 67–71
early 20th Century, 62–66, graph, 63
worldwide, 72–74, map, 72
Indiana, 205–208

I. Pages 62–66 are probably about
○ **A.** immigration in the 1950s.
○ **B.** immigration around 1900.
○ **C.** immigrants from Europe.
○ **D.** immigrants from Asia.

2. You would probably read about immigrants from Italy on pages
○ **A.** 45–50. ○ **C.** 72–74.
○ **B.** 51–54. ○ **D.** 41–44.

3. What does the book's map show?
○ **A.** immigration worldwide
○ **B.** Ellis Island
○ **C.** South America
○ **D.** immigration from Europe

4. Which page contains an illustration?
○ **A.** Page 205 ○ **C.** Page 69
○ **B.** Page 53 ○ **D.** Page 47

Reading Skills Practice Test 6

READING COMPREHENSION

Read each story. Then fill in the circle that best completes each sentence or answers each question.

Italy's Leaning Tower of Pisa was never straight. It started leaning before workers finished building it in the mid-1300s. Despite its **precarious** perch, the tower has maintained its tilt for 800 years. But all is not well with the tilting tower. These days, officials are worried that the eight-story tower could collapse.

I. The word **precarious** means
  ○ **A.** settled.
  ○ **B.** risky.
  ○ **C.** hilly.
  ○ **D.** previous.

2. Why are officials worried about the tower?
  ○ **A.** They are afraid it might collapse.
  ○ **B.** They think the tower is too old.
  ○ **C.** Workers never finished building it in the 1300s.
  ○ **D.** The town of Pisa was hit by an earthquake recently.

A. Contrary to popular belief, cracking your knuckles doesn't harm your joints, according to Dr. Thomas Trumble. He's a professor and surgeon at the University of Washington's division of hand and microvascular surgery in Seattle, Washington.

Dr. Trumble likens cracking your knuckles to "pulling a suction cup off a window." You don't harm the window or the suction cup at all. But you do hear a loud pop. The same is true for knuckles.

"All joints have a normal vacuum of air that helps them move smoothly," Dr. Trumble says. "When you crack your knuckles, you're just breaking that vacuum, so it doesn't do any harm at all. In fact, it feels good."

I. The purpose of this article is to
  ○ **A.** persuade you not to crack your knuckles.
  ○ **B.** tell you a funny story about knuckles.
  ○ **C.** explain what doctors do with knuckles.
  ○ **D.** inform you that cracking your knuckles is safe.

2. What is the best title for this story?
  ○ **A.** "Don't Crack Your Knuckles!"
  ○ **B.** "Crack Away!"
  ○ **C.** "All About the Knuckle"
  ○ **D.** "Some Popular Beliefs"

3. What does Dr. Trumble compare cracking your knuckles to?
  ○ **A.** cracking your joints
  ○ **B.** pulling a suction cup off a window
  ○ **C.** using a vacuum cleaner
  ○ **D.** eating something that makes loud pops

B. Two free lighters and free cigarettes. That's what Lara Coyne was promised in the mail. All she had to do was answer a tobacco company's survey questions about her smoking habits. Except Lara didn't smoke.

A high school senior in Rocky Mount, Virginia, Lara was only 16 years old. The legal age to buy cigarettes is 21. So when Lara received the offer for free cigarettes, her mother phoned a reporter. Lara quickly became the center of a story about the legal problems tobacco companies are now facing.

For years, cigarette makers have claimed they were not encouraging kids to smoke. But these days, tobacco executives have admitted that they have known for years that smoking is bad for your health. The press also discovered documents stating that some cigarette ads were aimed at teenagers.

l. What happened after Lara's mother called a reporter?
○ **A.** Lara became part of the tobacco companies' legal problems.
○ **B.** Lara took up smoking so she could get the free lighters.
○ **C.** Tobacco companies began aiming their ads at teenagers.
○ **D.** It was discovered that smoking is bad for your health.

2. This story might go on to talk about
○ **A.** Lara's family and friends.
○ **B.** the history of tobacco growing.
○ **C.** other things that are bad for your health.
○ **D.** details from the documents the press found.

C. Elisa Donovan found fame and fortune in Hollywood. This star of the TV show *Clueless* had a steady acting job, a good salary, and the opportunity to wear amazing clothes. But Elisa also had a secret. A secret that almost killed her. Elisa was anorexic. In 1995, she almost died.

"I never thought I would have to eat something or die," she says now. But that's exactly what happened. In the early 1990s, convinced that she needed to lose more and more weight, Elisa ate less and less food. By 1994, the 5-foot 6-inch actress weighed only 90 pounds.

Although she is healthy now, Elisa admits that she fears becoming anorexic again. The worst part of the disease, she says, is that anorexics live a secret life. "It's such a secret," she says. "All the rituals I would have with food were so secret. That's part of the disease." She's sharing her secret now in the hope that other girls might learn from her mistake and save themselves from this life-threatening illness.

l. In what year did Elisa almost die?
○ **A.** 1993.
○ **B.** 1994
○ **C.** 1995
○ **D.** 1996

2. What does Elisa think is the worst part of having anorexia?
○ **A.** eating too much
○ **B.** living a secret life
○ **C.** losing her TV job
○ **D.** feeling very powerful

3. Based on this story, you can conclude that
○ **A.** Elisa Donovan is not a very good actress.
○ **B.** Anorexia is not a serious disease.
○ **C.** It's very difficult to fully recover from anorexia.
○ **D.** Living a secret life is something to be admired.

D.   During World War II, German troops entered Havtan, Hungary, in March 1944. A few weeks later, they forced hundreds of Jews into a makeshift ghetto in a local sugar factory. Judith Kalman, 16, had to go there. Her mother did, too.

Soon after, Judith and her mother were deported to a prison camp. The Kalmans were among the 434,351 Jews sent to this particular concentration camp between May 15 and July 9, 1944. Most of the Hungarian Jews were gassed and killed soon after they arrived.

Judith was selected for slave labor. When told that her mother had been killed in the gas chambers, she refused to believe it. Judith was taken with 500 other inmates to an airplane factory in Germany. There, she cleared rubble from Allied bombing raids. She worked beside German factory workers. One of them brought Judith and another starving girl food every morning. This probably helped save her life.

On May 1, 1945, Judith was **liberated** from her prison camp. She weighed 48 pounds.

I.   What happens right after Judith and her mother are forced into the ghetto?
○ **A.** They are sent to a prison camp.
○ **B.** Judith is selected for slave labor.
○ **C.** A German worker gives Judith food.
○ **D.** Judith's prison camp is liberated.

2.   In this story, the word **liberated** means
○ **A.** hired.   ○ **C.** freed.
○ **B.** sold.   ○ **D.** killed.

3.   What might have helped save Judith's life?
○ **A.** the food the German worker gave her
○ **B.** the luxury of the prison camp
○ **C.** being in a ghetto first
○ **D.** always having her mother beside her

E.   Have you ever tried to write a poem? It's easier than you might think. Poems are a lot like song lyrics. A good poem reveals an honest feeling about something. Follow these steps to write a poem.

1. First, choose your topic. What would you like your poem to be about? Your poem will be more powerful if you choose a topic you feel strongly about.
2. Now freewrite for five minutes about your topic. Then go back and read it. Do any words or phrases stand out? Circle these to use in your poem.
3. Write your poem. Remember, a poem doesn't have to rhyme. It doesn't have to use sentences. But it should show your feelings about the topic. And it should sound nice to you.
4. Have a friend read your poem aloud to you. Do you like the way it sounds? If not, go back and rewrite the parts you don't like.
5. Enjoy your poem. Read it to others and to yourself. Post it somewhere if you want.

I.   To write a poem, what should you do first?
○ **A.** Freewrite.
○ **B.** Have a friend read a poem aloud.
○ **C.** Choose a topic.
○ **D.** Rewrite.

2.   In this article, what are poems compared to?
○ **A.** friends
○ **B.** freewriting
○ **C.** stories
○ **D.** song lyrics

3.   In which step of poetry writing do you rewrite?
○ **A.** 1
○ **B.** 2
○ **C.** 4
○ **D.** 5

VOCABULARY

Synonyms

Read the underlined word in each phrase. Mark the word below it that has the same (or close to the same) meaning.

Sample:

accurate measurement
- ○ **A.** large
- ○ **B.** precise
- ○ **C.** helpful
- ○ **D.** general

1. enable him
   - ○ **A.** follow
   - ○ **B.** imitate
   - ○ **C.** allow
   - ○ **D.** remind

2. gnarled limb
   - ○ **A.** twisted
   - ○ **B.** straight
   - ○ **C.** old
   - ○ **D.** dried

3. desperate plea
   - ○ **A.** screech
   - ○ **B.** request
   - ○ **C.** moan
   - ○ **D.** action

4. she was mute
   - ○ **A.** cute
   - ○ **B.** happy
   - ○ **C.** speechless
   - ○ **D.** awkward

5. rouse for work
   - ○ **A.** awaken
   - ○ **B.** hire
   - ○ **C.** interview
   - ○ **D.** invite

6. clash of ideas
   - ○ **A.** collision
   - ○ **B.** failure
   - ○ **C.** ruin
   - ○ **D.** downpour

7. revive hope
   - ○ **A.** survive
   - ○ **B.** reject
   - ○ **C.** renew
   - ○ **D.** provide

Antonyms

Read the bold word in each phrase. Mark the word below it that means the opposite or nearly the opposite.

Sample:

basic idea
- ○ **A.** simple
- ○ **B.** complicated
- ○ **C.** big
- ○ **D.** creative

1. coarse cloth
   - ○ **A.** fine
   - ○ **B.** heavy
   - ○ **C.** plain
   - ○ **D.** expensive

2. defend the accused
   - ○ **A.** help
   - ○ **B.** question
   - ○ **C.** free
   - ○ **D.** prosecute

3. complete misery
   - ○ **A.** happiness
   - ○ **B.** sadness
   - ○ **C.** freedom
   - ○ **D.** boredom

4. weird looking
   - ○ **A.** strange
   - ○ **B.** normal
   - ○ **C.** good
   - ○ **D.** awful

5. seldom done
   - ○ **A.** once
   - ○ **B.** always
   - ○ **C.** never
   - ○ **D.** often

6. gleeful yell
   - ○ **A.** joyous
   - ○ **B.** frightened
   - ○ **C.** loud
   - ○ **D.** unhappy

7. typical reaction
   - ○ **A.** usual
   - ○ **B.** unusual
   - ○ **C.** tired
   - ○ **D.** meaningless

READING COMPREHENSION

Read each story. Then fill in the circle that best completes each sentence or answers each question.

SAMPLE

When it comes to jumping, you might think frogs or kangaroos are the champs. Wrong! Grasshoppers have the greatest jumping ability of all animals in relation to their size. Grasshoppers can jump two feet high and four feet forward. That's equal to a human jumping over a tall building.

1. The best title for this story is
○ **A.** "Grasshoppers Are Super Jumpers"
○ **B.** "Frogs, Kangaroos and Grasshoppers"
○ **C.** "When Humans Jump Over Buildings"
○ **D.** "Grasshoppers Are Better Than People"

2. This author's point about grasshoppers is that
○ **A.** they can jump over buildings.
○ **B.** they can grow to be as tall as humans.
○ **C.** they can jump very high for how small they are.
○ **D.** they jump on only two feet.

A. Morgan White's lifelong dream was to compete in gymnastics in the Olympics. She fell in love with gymnastics at age five, after watching a competition on TV. She became a top American gymnast.

Morgan's favorite gymnastic event was the uneven bars. In it, a gymnast must move from a high bar to a low one with different swinging motions. Morgan was so good at this event that there's a gymnastic move named after her. The move, called "The White," involves a handstand and twist on the bars.

Becoming so good meant making many sacrifices. "All the girls in my group—we couldn't do after-school activities," said Morgan. "I couldn't stay up late because I had to get up for a workout early in the morning." But, she said, all the sacrifices were worth it.

1. What is the best title for this story?
○ **A.** "No After-School Activities"
○ **B.** "The Olympics"
○ **C.** "Gymnastics"
○ **D.** "Morgan White: Gymnast"

2. From this story, you can conclude that
○ **A.** Morgan worked very hard at gymnastics.
○ **B.** Morgan watched a lot of TV.
○ **C.** Boys do not do gymnastics.
○ **D.** Morgan only liked the uneven bars.

3. Why didn't Morgan stay up late?
○ **A.** Her parents didn't let her stay up late.
○ **B.** She was afraid of the dark.
○ **C.** She had to get her rest so that she could do gymnastics early in the morning.
○ **D.** Her friends didn't stay up late.

B. Karla Pierce was enjoying a springtime family barbecue in Skowhegan, Maine, when it happened. Her friend's dog, Tucker, accidentally fell into a nearby stream. The stream was thick with melted snow, and Tucker was heading straight for a dam.

Karla, 12, knew she had to be calm, stay focused, and act fast. She ran through some hay fields to the edge of the stream. Meanwhile, a few of the adults at the barbecue drove to the stream to reach Tucker before he got to the dam.

Karla got to the edge of the stream first. She hooked her foot around a small tree, and hung her body over the water to try and reach the dog. Kara could see that Tucker was fighting the water's current, or its movement, and was hitting some rocks. But Karla was able to grab Tucker by the front paws and, with some true muscle, pull him out of the stream.

I. This story is mostly about
   ○ **A.** how Karla saved her friend's dog, Tucker.
   ○ **B.** why water currents can be dangerous.
   ○ **C.** swimming dogs.
   ○ **D.** Karla Tucker's friends and family.

2. Which is a *fact*?
   ○ **A.** A dog should be kept on a leash.
   ○ **B.** Karla Tucker was brave to save her friend's dog.
   ○ **C.** A water's current means the speed of its movement.
   ○ **D.** Tucker was a lucky dog.

3. This story would probably go on to talk about
   ○ **A.** the history of dams.
   ○ **B.** food that Karla's family had been barbecuing.
   ○ **C.** springtime weather in Maine.
   ○ **D.** whether Tucker had been hurt or not.

C. The National Park Service (NPS) doesn't think the whooshing and whirring of snowmobiles belong with the beauty of nature. The NPS is already limiting the use of snowmobiles in national parks. Snowmobiles will be completely banned from Yellowstone and Grand Teton national parks by 2003. Yellowstone spreads out around the borders of Wyoming, Montana, and Idaho. Grant Teton is in Wyoming. Although the gas-fueled vehicles are a fun way to zip around on the snow, park officials say they're not good for the environment. The snowmobiles release harmful gases that pollute the air and harm wildlife, including bears and wolves.

I. What is the best title for this article?
   ○ **A.** "The Many Dangers of Snowmobiles"
   ○ **B.** "National Parks in the United States"
   ○ **C.** "NPS Limits the Use of Snowmobiles"
   ○ **D.** "Bears, Wolves, and Other Animals"

2. Which of these is an *opinion*?
   ○ **A.** Grand Teton is in Wyoming.
   ○ **B.** Snowmobiles are a fun way to zip around on the snow.
   ○ **C.** Snowmobiles are gas-fueled.
   ○ **D.** Snowmobiles pollute the air and harm wildlife.

3. The National Park Service is limiting the use of snowmobiles in national parks because
   ○ **A.** they release gases that hurt the environment.
   ○ **B.** they make noise which bothers bears and wolves.
   ○ **C.** they should only be ridden on the borders of Wyoming, Montana, and Idaho.
   ○ **D.** they are too expensive.

D. While pro wrestling isn't real, it isn't always safe either. That worries some experts, because the audience for pro wrestling includes a growing number of kids. Some kids **imitate** what their wrestling heros do and say, which can have fatal consequences. Police say a 3-year-old boy died in Texas when his 7-year-old brother used a wrestling move on him. Pediatrician Howard Spivak, an expert on kids and violence, thinks wrestling is poor entertainment for kids. "Pro wrestling not only shows inappropriate behavior, but shows that violence is an acceptable way of dealing with anger," he says.

Minnesota Governor Jesse Ventura, a former pro wrestler, doesn't think wrestling is any more violent than pro football or action movies. But he does think young kids should watch wrestling with their parents. Kids should also remember that pros train for months to learn how to fight safely.

"These are professionally trained people who know their art," Governor Ventura says.

1. Which of these is an *opinion* about wrestling?
   ○ **A.** Jesse Ventura is a former pro wrestler.
   ○ **B.** Wrestlers are professionally trained people.
   ○ **C.** Pro wrestling is fun to watch.
   ○ **D.** The audience for pro wrestling includes a growing number of kids.

2. In this article, the word **imitate** means
   ○ **A.** watch   ○ **C.** criticize
   ○ **B.** praise   ○ **D.** copy

3. You can conclude from this story that:
   ○ **A.** People have different opinions about whether kids should watch pro-wrestling.
   ○ **B.** Wrestling is good exercise.
   ○ **C.** Jesse Ventura left pro wrestling because he thought it was too violent.
   ○ **D.** Professional wrestlers never get hurt.

E. Imagine having your homework assignment become a state law. That's what happened to 10-year-old Katie McLean. She proposed a bill that was signed into law by Virginia Governor James Gilmore. The law **fines** people up to $250 if they litter in state parks.

How did it happen? Virginia lawmaker Kristen J. Admunson visited Katie's fourth-grade class at Stratford Elementary School in Alexandria, Virginia, and asked the class to write bill proposals as a homework assignment.

Katie chose to tackle littering. Admunson liked her idea, and the bill passed both the House of Delegates and the State Senate. The law took effect on July 1, 2001. Katie realized that kids can make a difference. "It made me think about what kids really can do," she said.

1. The purpose of Katie's bill was:
   ○ **A.** to take $250 from every person in Virginia.
   ○ **B.** to help prevent littering in state parks.
   ○ **C.** to show off.
   ○ **D.** to get to meet the Governor of Virginia.

2. In this passage, the word **fines** means
   ○ **A.** compliments.
   ○ **B.** gives.
   ○ **C.** sells.
   ○ **D.** punishes by taking a certain amount of money.

3. Which of the following had to happen in order for Katie's bill to become a state law?
   ○ **A.** It had to pass in the House of Delegates and the State Senate, and be signed into law by the Governor.
   ○ **B.** Virginia lawmaker Kristen J. Admunson had to pay $250.
   ○ **C.** Katie had to type the bill on a computer and send it to Governor James Gilmore.
   ○ **D.** Katie had to start middle school.

VOCABULARY

Synonyms

Read the underlined word in each phrase.
Mark the word below it that has the same
(or close to the same) meaning.

Sample:

exclude a classmate
- A. leave out
- C. excite
- B. hurt
- D. invite

1. appropriate behavior
   - A. late
   - C. proper
   - B. early
   - D. wrong

2. weather forecast
   - A. screen
   - C. person
   - B. prediction
   - D. show

3. animals are threatened
   - A. cute
   - C. in danger
   - B. fierce
   - D. lost

4. astonishing athlete
   - A. big
   - C. amazing
   - B. fast
   - D. aging

5. bawling infant
   - A. crying
   - C. eating
   - B. playing
   - D. sleeping

6. shapeless being
   - A. shapely
   - C. square
   - B. formless
   - D. strange

7. flurry of activity
   - A. burst
   - C. halt
   - B. end
   - D. lack

Antonyms

Read the underlined word in each phrase.
Mark the word below it that means the
opposite or nearly the opposite.

Sample:

snickering during the movie
- A. laughing
- C. eating
- B. crying
- D. watching

1. significant person
   - A. younger
   - C. unimportant
   - B. strong
   - D. friendly

2. unjustly accused
   - A. fairly
   - C. nearly
   - B. sadly
   - D. personally

3. stifle a groan
   - A. let out
   - C. keep in
   - B. try
   - D. whine

4. intentionally kicked
   - A. immediately
   - C. violently
   - B. accidentally
   - D. fortunately

5. approaching third
   - A. coming towards
   - C. falling over
   - B. watching
   - D. leaving

6. create chaos
   - A. order
   - C. action
   - B. disorder
   - D. understanding

7. hostile crowd
   - A. horrid
   - C. hysterical
   - B. futile
   - D. friendly

Reading Skills Practice Test 8

READING COMPREHENSION

Read each story. Then fill in the circle that best completes each sentence or answers each question.

SAMPLE

Ever wonder how much TV kids like you watch? Research shows that most American children watch three to five hours of TV every day. That's a lot. Is watching so much TV good or bad for kids?

Experts don't think watching TV is bad. They say that there are a lot of good shows for children. But they think it's important for kids to have better TV habits. Experts feel children should only watch one or two hours of TV a day.

1. According to the story, how much TV do most kids watch?
  ○ **A.** half an hour a day
  ○ **B.** one or two hours a day
  ○ **C.** three to five hours a day
  ○ **D.** more than five hours a day

2. What is the main idea of this story?
  ○ **A.** Kids don't watch enough TV.
  ○ **B.** Kids should watch one hour of TV a day.
  ○ **C.** Kids watch five hours of TV a day.
  ○ **D.** Kids should have better TV habits.

A.   When gum gets stuck in your hair, it can be an icky, sticky mess. Here are two good ways to get the gum out.

• The quickest way is to cut the gum out of your hair. However, this may not be the best way if you care a lot about your hairstyle. Your hair may end up looking strange, and it may take a while to grow back to normal.

• Another good way is to ease it out with some sort of oil. Try cooking oil or peanut butter. Just put a small amount of the oil or peanut butter in your hair and **knead** the gum between your fingers to soften it. As the gum softens, pull it out gently and slowly.

1.   What is the best title for this story?
  ○ **A.** "The Perks of Peanut Butter"
  ○ **B.** "Getting the Gum Out"
  ○ **C.** "Horrible Hairstyles"
  ○ **D.** "Growing Out Your Hair"

2.   In this story, the word **knead** means
  ○ **A.** need.
  ○ **B.** want.
  ○ **C.** press gently.
  ○ **D.** punch hard.

3.   What is the similarity between the two ways of getting gum out of your hair?
  ○ **A.** They both work.
  ○ **B.** They both ruin your hairstyle.
  ○ **C.** They both use peanut butter.
  ○ **D.** They both use scissors.

B. The next time you cool off with an ice-cold Popsicle, you can thank Frank Epperson. He was just 11 years old when he came up with this famous frozen treat. Here is what happened.

In 1905, young Frank mixed together some powdered soda pop to drink. He left the cup on the back porch overnight with the stirring stick still in it.

When Frank went out to the porch the next morning, he found a stick of frozen soda water. He brought it to school that day. Soon, he was selling his creation to friends.

The rest, as they say, is history. When Frank grew up, he patented his invention and named it the Popsicle. By 1928, more than 60 million Popsicles had been sold.

I. From this story you can guess that
○ **A.** Frank didn't like soda pop.
○ **B.** it was very cold the night Frank left his soda pop out.
○ **C.** Frank's friends thought the frozen soda pop tasted awful.
○ **D.** Frank's mother is responsible for the invention of Popsicles.

2. Which of these adjectives best describes Frank Epperson?
○ **A.** lazy   ○ **C.** habitual
○ **B.** silly   ○ **D.** ambitious

3. The purpose of this story is to
○ **A.** inform you about the invention of Popsicles.
○ **B.** entertain you with Frank's story.
○ **C.** persuade you that Popsicles are delicious.
○ **D.** warn you that Popsicles are bad.

C. Imagine a wall of water as high as a 12-story building. What if one hit the coast of the United States? Some scientists think this could happen. They think the Northwest U.S. could be hit by this giant wave, called a tsunami (soo-nah-mee). This area could be threatened because it is across the ocean from the Far East. That's where earthquakes create the largest tsunamis.

That's why scientists are testing a new machine. The machine will warn people about these waves—before they hit. When people don't know that a tsunami is coming, it can be deadly. For instance, a monster wave hit the island of New Guinea and killed 2,200 people.

It is hoped that machines placed on the ocean floor will be able to measure the size of the waves. People will then know when they have to **flee** the coast because a big wave is on the way!

I. The Northwest is a possible tsunami site because
○ **A.** it is on the coast.
○ **B.** it is close to New Guinea.
○ **C.** it is across the ocean from the Far East.
○ **D.** its ocean is very deep.

2. In this story, the word **flee** means
○ **A.** run away.   ○ **C.** destroy.
○ **B.** move toward.   ○ **D.** protect.

3. How are scientists hoping to protect people against tsunamis?
○ **A.** by preventing tsunamis from happening
○ **B.** by using a machine that will warn people about tsunamis
○ **C.** by keeping people from living in the Northwest
○ **D.** by making the tsunamis into smaller waves

D. There were once two neighbors named Chen and Li. Chen was a rich man, but very unhappy. He worried about money constantly. Li was poor, but happy. He had few worries. Each night, Li's house was filled with laughing and singing.

One day, Chen invited Li to his house. "I am giving you 500 silver pieces to start your own business," he announced. "Even though you will become rich, do not pay me back." Li was shocked. He did not want to be rich. He knew that money caused worry. But he thanked Chen for his generosity and went home.

For the next few nights, there was no joy at Li's house. Li could not stop worrying about how to use the money. He could hardly sleep.

Finally, after several days, Li returned to Chen's house. He gave the money back and immediately felt relieved. He went home and ate dinner. He slept soundly the whole night through. And the next night, Li's house was filled with laughing and singing again.

I. What is Li's problem in this story?
○ **A.** He doesn't have enough money.
○ **B.** He is not very happy.
○ **C.** He doesn't like to sleep or eat.
○ **D.** He's given what he doesn't want.

2. How does Li solve his problem?
○ **A.** He makes a lot of money.
○ **B.** He sings and laughs.
○ **C.** He sleeps late and eats a lot.
○ **D.** He gives the money back.

3. What is the moral of this story?
○ **A.** Money makes you happy.
○ **B.** Money doesn't bring happiness.
○ **C.** Good neighbors don't give money to each other.
○ **D.** Good neighbors laugh and sing together.

E. Mosquito bites are not just itchy and annoying. Now, in the United States, a rare kind of virus carried by certain mosquitoes may cause serious illness. In some extreme cases, it may even lead to death.

In the summer of 1999, people in New York City and surrounding areas learned about a new virus. It was caused by the bites of certain mosquitoes. Experts believe these mosquitoes carry a form of the West Nile virus. Before 1999, this dangerous virus had never been found in the United States.

Most people infected with West Nile virus have no symptoms. Some, however, do get a fever and a headache. And some fall seriously ill. They have to be hospitalized.

The best defense against the West Nile virus is preventing mosquito bites. What's the best protection from these nasty insects? Wear long-sleeved shirts and long pants. And keep the insect repellent close at hand!

I. What is the best title for this story?
○ **A.** "The West Nile Virus"
○ **B.** "How to Treat Mosquito Bites"
○ **C.** "Annoying Insects"
○ **D.** "Protecting Yourself From Bites"

2. Which of the following is an *opinion*?
○ **A.** Some mosquitoes carry a dangerous virus.
○ **B.** Many people infected with West Nile virus have no symptoms.
○ **C.** Mosquito bites are so itchy and annoying.
○ **D.** Preventing mosquito bites helps prevent West Nile virus.

3. From this story you can conclude that
○ **A.** everyone in New York is in mortal danger.
○ **B.** in New York, mosquito bites are more dangerous than they used to be.
○ **C.** all mosquitoes are deadly.
○ **D.** people should never go outside unless they are wrapped from head to toe.

VOCABULARY
Which Word Is Missing?

In each of the following passages, a words is missing. First, read each passages Then choose the missing word from the list beneath the passage. Fill in the circle next to the word that is missing.

Sample:

Last night, Shawn's parents dragged him to the world's most boring movie. He sat in his seat, waiting for it to be over, but the film seemed _____.

- ○ **A.** fascinating
- ○ **B.** terrible
- ○ **C.** endless
- ○ **D.** brief

I. When Aysha first hurt her wrist, she was in _____. The pain was unbearable.
- ○ **A.** ecstasy
- ○ **B.** mourning
- ○ **C.** denial
- ○ **D.** agony

2. Fortunately, it wasn't broken. "I could have _____ worse," she said to herself.
- ○ **A.** fared
- ○ **B.** expanded
- ○ **C.** ranged
- ○ **D.** read

3. She did, however, have to wear a cast for two weeks. She knew she could _____. After all, two weeks wasn't very much.
- ○ **A.** cry
- ○ **B.** survive
- ○ **C.** consent
- ○ **D.** grieve

4. Her friends all signed her cast. They used _____ colors so the signatures would stand out.
- ○ **A.** subtle
- ○ **B.** faint
- ○ **C.** large
- ○ **D.** vivid

5. When the cast came off, Aysha was a little _____. It had become such a part of herself, she almost wanted it back.
- ○ **A.** wistful
- ○ **B.** eager
- ○ **C.** dreary
- ○ **D.** grateful

6. Most people think it's _____ to have soup for dessert. But I don't. I think it's perfectly normal.
- ○ **A.** ordinary
- ○ **B.** exciting
- ○ **C.** peculiar
- ○ **D.** irritating

7. I don't like sweets that much. But I do want something _____ after dinner. For me, soup fits the bill.
- ○ **A.** enjoyable
- ○ **B.** bitter
- ○ **C.** tasteless
- ○ **D.** elaborate

8. The appearance of a bowl of _____ soup always makes me happy. My nose fills with delicious odors.
- ○ **A.** ordinary
- ○ **B.** greasy
- ○ **C.** murky
- ○ **D.** fragrant

9. My father has been making me soup for dessert for many years. He gets _____ if anyone makes fun of my unique choice of after-dinner treat.
- ○ **A.** petrified
- ○ **B.** indignant
- ○ **C.** unsure
- ○ **D.** childish

10. Sometimes my friends can't help but _____ when my dad places a big bowl of steaming chowder in front of me—especially when they're having chocolate cake!
- ○ **A.** grandstand
- ○ **B.** snicker
- ○ **C.** babble
- ○ **D.** rejoice

Reading Skills Practice Test 9

READING COMPREHENSION

Read each story. Then fill in the circle that best completes each sentence or answers each question.

There's no doubt about it. The world's most popular sport isn't basketball or baseball. It's soccer. Soccer is watched and played by far more people. Soccer's **astounding** popularity is shown by the size of the television audience for the World Cup. The World Cup is soccer's championship. Almost 1.5 billion people watched the 1998 World Cup final. The number grew to 3.2 billion in 2010, and even more in 2014!

I. In this passage the word **astounding** means
○ **A.** lack of.
○ **B.** amazing.
○ **C.** disappearing.
○ **D.** different.

2. What is the best title for this story?
○ **A.** "Soccer—The World's Favorite Sport"
○ **B.** "Soccer in America"
○ **C.** "Popular Television Programs"
○ **D.** "Baseball and Soccer Are My Favorite Games"

A. Have you ever heard a haiku? A haiku is a type of short poem that developed in Japan. Each haiku has only three lines and 17 syllables. The first and last lines have five syllables each. The second line has seven syllables.

Because of its small size, a haiku doesn't express long, complicated ideas. Usually, it simply tries to capture a single moment in time. Still, haiku is a very powerful form of poetry. Often, the subject is nature.

Although haiku developed years ago, the form is still popular in modern Japan. Many people make a hobby of composing haiku. Haiku clubs and magazines are also very popular.

I. How many syllables does a haiku contain?
○ **A.** 5
○ **B.** 7
○ **C.** 15
○ **D.** 17

2. You can conclude from this story that
○ **A.** Haikus are not as popular as they were in the past.
○ **B.** Every haiku contains images from nature.
○ **C.** Long poems are more interesting.
○ **D.** Haiku was developed in Japan.

B.   The Tyrannosaurus rex (T. rex) roamed North America about 65 million years ago. For years, it was thought of as the king of meat-eating dinosaurs. It was a truly massive animal. It grew to 40 feet in length and weighed as much as 7 tons. Recently, however, a new dino has been discovered. Its name is Giganotosaurus. It may be the real "king" dinosaur.

The discovery occurred in Argentina. Scientists found the fossils of the new dinosaur in the southern part of the country. Judging by its skeleton, the Giganotosaurus appears to outweigh the T. rex by as many as 3 tons. It may have been over 45 feet in length. The Giganotosaurus is also an older dinosaur. It lived about 100 million years ago.

I.   The purpose of this article is to
   ○ **A.** amuse.   ○ **C.** persuade.
   ○ **B.** inform.   ○ **D.** sell a product.

2.   What happened most recently?
   ○ **A.** The Giganotosaurus roamed the earth.
   ○ **B.** The Giganotosaurus was discovered.
   ○ **C.** The Tyrannosaurus roamed the earth.
   ○ **D.** The Tyrannosaurus was discovered.

3.   You can conclude from this article that
   ○ **A.** scientists will never discover a bigger dinosaur than the Giganotosaurus.
   ○ **B.** scientists have learned everything there is to know about the Giganotosaurus.
   ○ **C.** scientists are still learning important things about dinosaurs.
   ○ **D.** T-rex and the Giganotosaurus were about the same weight.

C.   No one had tried to break the window. It was simply an accident. Rosemary and Leslie were playing basketball in front of Rosemary's garage. As usual, Leslie had won.

It wasn't that Rosemary wasn't a skilled basketball player. In fact, she was exceptionally talented. She had a superior jump shot. She could dribble equally well with both hands. She was accomplished at grabbing rebounds. The trouble was that she easily became distracted. In the middle of a game she would see a neighbor's automobile drive by and instead of **concentrating** on playing basketball, she would wave to say hello. Sometimes, in the middle of taking a shot, she would begin thinking about what she wanted for dinner.

Anyway, after the game was finished, Leslie threw the ball to Rosemary. As usual, however, Rosemary was thinking about something else. The ball sailed straight past her and through the living-room window.

"Oh no!" shouted Leslie. "We have to go and explain to your parents."

"You're right," said Rosemary. "Let's find them before they come to us."

I.   In this story, the word **concentrating** means
   ○ **A.** hesitating.
   ○ **B.** forgetting about.
   ○ **C.** focusing on.
   ○ **D.** counting on.

2.   According to the story, why does Leslie usually win games with Rosemary?
   ○ **A.** Rosemary always gets distracted.
   ○ **B.** Rosemary isn't very talented.
   ○ **C.** Rosemary is very talented.
   ○ **D.** Leslie is extremely talented.

3.   How does Leslie seem to feel about the accident?
   ○ **A.** thrilled.   ○ **C.** happy.
   ○ **B.** upset.   ○ **D.** bored.

4.   The next paragraph is likely to be about
   ○ **A.** Rosemary's new neighbor.
   ○ **B.** Leslie's favorite activities.
   ○ **C.** how Leslie learned to play basketball.
   ○ **D.** how Rosemary's parents react to the accident.

D. The Galápagos Islands are a special place. Located 600 miles from Ecuador's coast, they have all kinds of wildlife. About 5,000 species of plants and animals call the islands home. Many are unique. Animals like the Galápagos tortoise exist nowhere else in the world.

Sadly, some of these species are in danger. For example, the tortoise population has shrunk from 250,000 to less than 15,000. The number of sea lions has shrunk, too. So has the number of birds.

There are many different reasons why this wildlife is threatened. One reason is tourism. Since the 1960s, people have flocked to the islands. They come to see tortoises, iguanas, and penguins.

Today, about 65,000 tourists arrive every year. The crowds put stress on the fragile habitat. Their boats bring insects and other pests. These pests can harm the islands' native species.

I. The main idea of this article is that
  ○ **A.** The unique wildlife of the Galápagos is endangered.
  ○ **B.** Insects can harm the islands' native species.
  ○ **C.** The Galápagos are located off Ecuador's coast.
  ○ **D.** One reason is tourism.

2. Which of these is an *opinion*?
  ○ **A.** There are 15,000 tortoises.
  ○ **B.** There were 250,000 tortoises.
  ○ **C.** The number of sea lions has shrunk.
  ○ **D.** The Galápagos are special.

3. You can infer from this story that
  ○ **A.** Wildlife is the main attraction for visitors to the Galápagos.
  ○ **B.** The tortoise population will soon grow larger.
  ○ **C.** It used to be easier to get to the islands.
  ○ **D.** The tortoises rarely eat birds.

E. Have you ever thought about taking a long bike trip? These trips can be a lot of fun. Keep in mind, however, that you'll need to bring along the proper equipment. Carrying the essentials can mean the difference between a great trip and a bad one.

The most important piece of equipment is a helmet, naturally. A helmet will help to keep you safe if an accident occurs. A good helmet should fit snugly onto your head. A helmet that fits improperly might not provide you with sufficient protection. Other important items are a spare inner tube, a compact pump, and a multitool set. If you're in a distant place when a tire goes flat or a spoke comes loose, you'll be happy to have brought them along.

I. A helmet that doesn't fit properly
  ○ **A.** will usually protect the rider.
  ○ **B.** won't be as comfortable for the rider.
  ○ **C.** might not provide protection in an accident.
  ○ **D.** is an important piece of equipment.

2. The purpose of this article is to
  ○ **A.** make you laugh at how funny bike trips are.
  ○ **B.** inform you about what to bring on a bike trip.
  ○ **C.** persuade you not to go on bike trips.
  ○ **D.** tell you a story about a bike trip.

3. Which of the following is an *opinion*?
  ○ **A.** Long bike trips are fun.
  ○ **B.** A helmet can help keep you safe.
  ○ **C.** A helmet must fit properly to protect you.
  ○ **D.** A pump will be useful in case of a flat.

VOCABULARY

Synonyms

Read the underlined word in each phrase. Mark the word below it that has the same (or close to the same) meaning.

Sample:

sole survivor
- ○ **A.** only
- ○ **B.** lucky
- ○ **C.** large
- ○ **D.** silly

1. conceal the evidence
   - ○ **A.** display
   - ○ **B.** contribute
   - ○ **C.** protect
   - ○ **D.** hide

2. from another era
   - ○ **A.** place
   - ○ **B.** story
   - ○ **C.** time period
   - ○ **D.** community

3. beg to differ
   - ○ **A.** gather
   - ○ **B.** disagree
   - ○ **C.** remain
   - ○ **D.** be forgiven

4. cherish the moment
   - ○ **A.** forget
   - ○ **B.** detect
   - ○ **C.** disgrace
   - ○ **D.** treasure

5. hair-raising situation
   - ○ **A.** terrifying
   - ○ **B.** thrilling
   - ○ **C.** hilarious
   - ○ **D.** fast-moving

6. supreme confidence
   - ○ **A.** absolute
   - ○ **B.** little
   - ○ **C.** surprising
   - ○ **D.** inadequate

7. acquire knowledge
   - ○ **A.** lose
   - ○ **B.** gain
   - ○ **C.** reject
   - ○ **D.** reflect

Antonyms

Read the underlined word in each phrase. Mark the word below it that means the opposite or nearly the opposite.

Sample:

create chaos
- ○ **A.** chatter
- ○ **B.** noise
- ○ **C.** disturbance
- ○ **D.** order

1. a flimsy excuse
   - ○ **A.** unbelievable
   - ○ **B.** early
   - ○ **C.** late
   - ○ **D.** solid

2. oppose the motion
   - ○ **A.** tighten
   - ○ **B.** support
   - ○ **C.** cease
   - ○ **D.** oppress

3. considerable expense
   - ○ **A.** costly
   - ○ **B.** worthwhile
   - ○ **C.** unfortunate
   - ○ **D.** insignificant

4. appropriate action
   - ○ **A.** fast
   - ○ **B.** unsuitable
   - ○ **C.** discouraging
   - ○ **D.** brazen

5. vague idea
   - ○ **A.** precise
   - ○ **B.** vacant
   - ○ **C.** unclear
   - ○ **D.** uneven

6. betray the cause
   - ○ **A.** disturb
   - ○ **B.** believe
   - ○ **C.** support
   - ○ **D.** understand

7. reckless behavior
   - ○ **A.** careless
   - ○ **B.** careful
   - ○ **C.** proud
   - ○ **D.** humble

Reading Skills Practice Test 10

READING COMPREHENSION

Read each story. Then fill in the circle that best completes each sentence or answers each question.

Victoria Falls is the world's most amazing waterfall. It is almost a mile wide. Two countries share Victoria Falls: Zimbabwe and Zambia. At the falls, the Zambezi River flows over a cliff. Thirty million gallons of water pass by each minute. The drop is 350 feet. The falling water creates an enormous roar. People can hear the sound over 20 miles away.

I. What is the best title for this story?
○ **A.** "Zimbabwe and Zambia"
○ **B.** "The Mighty Victoria Falls"
○ **C.** "Sounds People Hear"
○ **D.** "Waterfalls of the World"

2. Which of these is an *opinion*?
○ **A.** It is almost a mile wide.
○ **B.** Two countries share the falls.
○ **C.** Victoria Falls is the world's most amazing waterfall.
○ **D.** Thirty million gallons of water pass by each minute.

A. The oldest organized sport in North America is a game called lacrosse.

Lacrosse has been played for hundreds of years. It was invented by Native Americans in Eastern Canada who called it *baggattaway*. Like baseball or football, lacrosse is an outdoor sport. The game's object is to send a ball into a goal using a special stick. The stick looks like a tennis racket, but it isn't flat. At the stick's end is a webbed pocket. The pocket is used to carry, pass, and catch the ball.

Lacrosse is played by two teams with 10 players on a side. The positions are much like the positions in soccer. There are defenders, goalkeepers, and midfielders. As in soccer, only the goalkeeper is allowed to touch the ball with his hands.

I. The game called *baggattaway* was
○ **A.** invented in the Eastern United States.
○ **B.** invented after basketball.
○ **C.** invented in Eastern Canada.
○ **D.** never played in Canada.

2. The purpose of this article is to
○ **A.** persuade you to play lacrosse.
○ **B.** inform you about a sport.
○ **C.** warn you about sports injuries.
○ **D.** amuse you with a funny sports story.

B.   Eight dollars a ticket? Ten dollars a ticket? Fourteen dollars a ticket? Everyone loves movies, but how much is too much when it comes to price? Going to see a film has become more expensive. In some cities, it can cost more than sixty dollars to take a family of four to the cinema—if you include overpriced popcorn and soda.

People in the movie business say that the cost of a ticket is still **reasonable**. They argue that ticket prices reflect the growing costs of making films. A big Hollywood blockbuster can cost over $300 million. Actors' salaries, and special effects, make up a big part of that expense.

Audiences may grumble when they have to pay more, but it hasn't kept them from filling theaters: ticket sales continue to rise.

I. In this article, the word **reasonable** means
   ○ **A.** fair.   ○ **C.** unjust.
   ○ **B.** expensive.   ○ **D.** irregular.

2. Which of these is a *fact*?
   ○ **A.** Everyone loves movies.
   ○ **B.** Ten dollars is too much to pay for a movie ticket.
   ○ **C.** The cost of a ticket is reasonable.
   ○ **D.** Blockbuster movies can cost over $300 million to make.

3. According to people in the movie business, why are ticket prices rising?
   ○ **A.** People are willing to pay any amount for a ticket.
   ○ **B.** Films are more expensive to make.
   ○ **C.** Actors don't earn very much money.
   ○ **D.** All films include expensive special effects.

C.   Dinosaurs no longer walk the planet, but there's one animal that comes close. It's called the Komodo dragon, and it's the largest lizard in the world.

There are about 6,000 of these monster reptiles. They live on a few small islands in Indonesia. A full-grown dragon can weigh 250 pounds and reach 10 feet in length. To reach this size, it eats all kinds of animals. Rats, birds, deer, and even water buffalo are food for the Komodo dragon.

People who live on the islands try to stay out of the dragon's path. Sometimes, the lizard will attack humans.

Historians believe that these lizards inspired myths and folktales about fire-breathing dragons. While they don't really breathe fire, their bite is very poisonous. An animal that is bitten by a Komodo dragon almost always dies.

I. When fully grown, a Komodo dragon
   ○ **A.** can breathe fire.
   ○ **B.** will not eat a water buffalo.
   ○ **C.** can weigh as much as 250 pounds.
   ○ **D.** will always attack humans.

2. You can infer from this article that
   ○ **A.** Komodo dragons usually live for 15 years or longer.
   ○ **B.** Komodo dragons are a type of dinosaur.
   ○ **C.** historians are not very interested in Komodo dragons.
   ○ **D.** scientists who study the dragons have to be very careful.

3. The best title for this story is
   ○ **A.** "Indonesian Reptiles."
   ○ **B.** "Indonesia's Komodo Dragons."
   ○ **C.** "Dragons That Breath Fire."
   ○ **D.** "Dragon Myths and Legends."

D. Technology has changed the way we walk in the woods. In the past, hikers would carry compasses to avoid getting lost. These days, wilderness lovers are more likely to carry GPS devices. GPS stands for *global positioning system.* The first GPS devices were tiny radios that communicated with satellites. Now, cell phones have GPS apps. They find your location and display it on a screen. A GPS device can tell you exactly where you are, anywhere on the earth.

The most amazing thing about GPS devices is their size and their accuracy. They are incredibly small, but such a big help if you get lost in the woods. GPS began in the 1970s. It was an invention of the U.S. Department of Defense. The department launched 24 satellites into orbit. For years, only the military used these satellites. Now, of course, they're **available** for everyone, and they can locate you anywhere.

I. The main purpose of this story is to
   ○ **A.** persuade.   ○ **C.** warn.
   ○ **B.** amuse.   ○ **D.** inform.

2. In this story, the word **available** means
   ○ **A.** automatic.   ○ **C.** accessible.
   ○ **B.** free.   ○ **D.** additional.

3. According to the article, GPS devices have replaced
   ○ **A.** satellites.   ○ **C.** phones.
   ○ **B.** compasses.   ○ **D.** radios.

E. It takes a special potato to make great fries. That's one thing America's top chefs agree on. These expert cooks know that there are all kinds of potatoes, and each kind is good for a specific purpose. Russet potatoes, for example, are great for baking. Red potatoes are best when boiled. White potatoes are tastiest in potato salad.

The chefs also agree that potatoes are very nutritious. Potatoes contain protein and many vitamins. A single potato provides 50 percent of the daily requirement for vitamin C. In fact, potatoes, like lemons, were once prized by sailors. Vitamin C prevents scurvy. On long ocean voyages, eating potatoes helped seafarers avoid getting the disease.

To get the most nutrients out of a potato, listen to the chefs. They say to cook potatoes with the skin on. Vitamins are lost when potatoes are peeled before cooking.

One thing the chefs can't agree on is where the best potatoes are grown. Some say Washington. Others say Idaho. One **maintains** that it is Wisconsin.

I. In this article, the word **maintains** means
   ○ **A.** knows.
   ○ **B.** argues.
   ○ **C.** repeats.
   ○ **D.** reacts.

2. According to the article, sailors ate potatoes because
   ○ **A.** potatoes help prevent a disease.
   ○ **B.** potatoes taste delicious.
   ○ **C.** potatoes contain protein.
   ○ **D.** russet potatoes are great for baking.

3. Which of these is a *fact*?
   ○ **A.** It takes a special potato to make great fries.
   ○ **B.** Red potatoes are best when boiled.
   ○ **C.** One potato provides 50 percent of the daily requirement for vitamin C.
   ○ **D.** The best potatoes are grown in Washington.

VOCABULARY

Synonyms

Read the underlined word in each phrase. Mark the word below it that has the same (or close to the same) meaning.

Sample:

    <u>linger</u> around
- ○ **A.** run
- ○ **B.** jump
- ○ **C.** look
- ○ **D.** wait

1.   desert <u>isle</u>
   - ○ **A.** aisle
   - ○ **B.** island
   - ○ **C.** lily
   - ○ **D.** while

2.   <u>precise</u> drawing
   - ○ **A.** quick
   - ○ **B.** accurate
   - ○ **C.** humorous
   - ○ **D.** realistic

3.   time to <u>rejoice</u>
   - ○ **A.** relate
   - ○ **B.** celebrate
   - ○ **C.** examine
   - ○ **D.** spend

4.   look <u>longingly</u>
   - ○ **A.** patiently
   - ○ **B.** hungrily
   - ○ **C.** mentally
   - ○ **D.** spitefully

5.   <u>sincere</u> remark
   - ○ **A.** awful
   - ○ **B.** friendly
   - ○ **C.** unexpected
   - ○ **D.** honest

6.   <u>fabulous</u> recipe
   - ○ **A.** excellent
   - ○ **B.** tasteless
   - ○ **C.** difficult
   - ○ **D.** frivolous

7.   <u>humiliating</u> event
   - ○ **A.** successful
   - ○ **B.** embarrassing
   - ○ **C.** disturbing
   - ○ **D.** frightening

Antonyms

Read the underlined word in each phrase. Mark the word below it that means the opposite or nearly the opposite.

Sample:

    <u>hard-working</u> fellow
- ○ **A.** lazy
- ○ **B.** active
- ○ **C.** smart
- ○ **D.** humble

1.   <u>prehistoric</u> cave
   - ○ **A.** frightening
   - ○ **B.** damp
   - ○ **C.** ancient
   - ○ **D.** modern

2.   <u>fragile</u> instrument
   - ○ **A.** heavy
   - ○ **B.** dangerous
   - ○ **C.** costly
   - ○ **D.** unbreakable

3.   <u>captive</u> prisoner
   - ○ **A.** powerful
   - ○ **B.** civil
   - ○ **C.** disgraceful
   - ○ **D.** escaped

4.   <u>attract</u> flies
   - ○ **A.** repel
   - ○ **B.** swat
   - ○ **C.** beckon
   - ○ **D.** avoid

5.   awful <u>uproar</u>
   - ○ **A.** election
   - ○ **B.** performance
   - ○ **C.** flavor
   - ○ **D.** silence

6.   <u>artificial</u> flavoring
   - ○ **A.** superficial
   - ○ **B.** delicious
   - ○ **C.** unusual
   - ○ **D.** natural

7.   <u>overtake</u> the leader
   - ○ **A.** overwhelm
   - ○ **B.** obstruct
   - ○ **C.** fall behind
   - ○ **D.** rejoin

READING COMPREHENSION

Read each story. Then fill in the circle that best completes each sentence or answers each question.

People say a good pair of shoes will last a long time. How about 8,000 years? That's how old some Native American shoes found in a Missouri cave are. About 35 shoes have been found in the cave. Of course, none of them have Velcro straps or air-cushion soles. And they're not made of leather or nylon, either. Most of them are made of rattlesnake master, a tough, spiny desert plant.

I. What is the best title for this story?
○ **A.** "In the Cave"
○ **B.** "Really Old Shoes"
○ **C.** "Fifty Years of Shoes"
○ **D.** "Shoes With Velcro"

2. What are the shoes in the cave made of?
○ **A.** leather
○ **B.** nylon
○ **C.** snakeskin
○ **D.** rattlesnake master

A. Did you know that giant otters live in South America's Amazon region? These water-loving creatures can grow as long as six feet. They **prowl** the Amazon in packs. Banding together helps them hunt for fish and protect their babies from crocodiles.

Giant otters also speak their own unique language. Whistles, whines, squeals, and snorts are all part of the otter's vocabulary. Each sound means a different thing. If a giant otter thinks a human hunter is getting too close, it will snort "pffttt!" This sound warns other otters of danger.

Giant otters have to warn each other a lot. Because of hunting, there are now only about 4,000 of these creatures left.

I. How do giant otters warn each other about hunters?
○ **A.** They snort.
○ **B.** They squeal.
○ **C.** They whistle.
○ **D.** They whine.

2. In this story, the word **prowl** means
○ **A.** live.
○ **B.** die.
○ **C.** move through.
○ **D.** collect.

3. Why are there only 4,000 giant otters left?
○ **A.** The crocodiles have eaten many of them.
○ **B.** Many of them have been hunted.
○ **C.** Their language is very hard to learn.
○ **D.** The Amazon region is being polluted.

B. In Bunol, Spain, the term "food fight" takes on a whole new meaning. Bunol is the site of an **annual** tomato fight, known as the *Tomatina*.

Each year, on the last Wednesday in August, the people of Bunol pelt each other with tomatoes. About 20,000 people take part. Many of them are kids. Over 240,000 pounds of tomatoes are thrown.

After the fight ends, the town is covered in tomato juice, pulp, and seeds. But the mess isn't left for someone else to take care of. The fighters who made the mess actually get together to clean it up.

They don't make tomato sauce with what remains on the streets of their town. They just return the streets to their original state.

I. How many tomatoes are used in the tomato fight?
- ○ **A.** 20 pounds
- ○ **B.** 200 pounds
- ○ **C.** 20,000 pounds
- ○ **D.** 240,000 pounds

2. In this story, the word **annual** means
- ○ **A.** large.
- ○ **B.** amazing.
- ○ **C.** yearly.
- ○ **D.** monthly.

3. What is the best title for this story?
- ○ **A.** "A Real Food Fight"
- ○ **B.** "All About Tomatoes"
- ○ **C.** "Bunol—A Quiet Town"
- ○ **D.** "Spanish Food"

C. Everyone knows Razor scooters are very popular. Lots of kids have them. In fact, millions of these scooters have been sold in the U.S.

Unfortunately, the rise in scooter sales has also meant a rise in scooter injuries. Over 50,000 scooter-related injuries were reported in 2013. Many of them could have been prevented with a few scooter safety tips. They are:
- Always wear protection when you ride a scooter. A helmet, knee pads, and elbow pads will help protect you.
- Always ride your scooter in a safe place. Don't ride near car traffic or on steep hills.
- Don't let your younger sibling borrow your scooter. Kids under the age of 8 shouldn't ride scooters without an adult **present**.

If you follow these tips you'll be a safe scooter rider.

I. The purpose of this story is to
- ○ **A.** inform you about scooter safety.
- ○ **B.** entertain you with scooter stories.
- ○ **C.** persuade you to buy a scooter.
- ○ **D.** warn you not to buy a scooter.

2. In this story, the word **present** means
- ○ **A.** gift.
- ○ **B.** now.
- ○ **C.** right there.
- ○ **D.** teacher.

3. What contributed to a rise in scooter-related injuries?
- ○ **A.** wearing helmets
- ○ **B.** a rise in scooter sales
- ○ **C.** riding scooters in safe places
- ○ **D.** riding scooters with adults

D. **Carlos:** Did you watch the basketball game last night?

Sam: Sure. I couldn't believe it when Carter went in for that dunk. It was amazing!

Carlos: I missed that part. How'd he do it?

Sam: Well, first he caught a pass from the point guard. Then, he dribbled towards the hoop. And then, he flew up from about five feet away and slammed the ball home.

Carlos: He's really an incredible player.

Sam: Yeah, I'll say. I wish I could dunk like that.

Carlos: Me too. But coach says I'll have to grow a few inches first.

Sam: You and me both. I guess now we should get dressed and go to practice.

1. Which of these is a *fact*?
- ⭘ **A.** Carter is an incredible player.
- ⭘ **B.** Carter's dunk was amazing.
- ⭘ **C.** Carter slammed the ball home.
- ⭘ **D.** Carter's dunk was unbelievable.

2. During his dunk, which of the following did Carter do second?
- ⭘ **A.** catch a pass from the point guard
- ⭘ **B.** dribble towards the hoop
- ⭘ **C.** take off from five feet away
- ⭘ **D.** slam the ball home

3. Based on the passage, which of the following statements is probably true?
- ⭘ **A.** Carlos and Sam are both very tall.
- ⭘ **B.** Carlos and Sam are on the same basketball team.
- ⭘ **C.** Carlos and Sam play basketball as well as Carter.
- ⭘ **D.** Carlos and Sam don't like basketball very much.

4. How is Carter different from Carlos and Sam?
- ⭘ **A.** He's short.
- ⭘ **B.** He plays basketball.
- ⭘ **C.** He's a guy.
- ⭘ **D.** He can dunk well.

E. At 29,028 feet, the peak of Mount Everest is the highest place on Earth. It used to be a tough place to get to. Everest is set deep in the Himalayan Mountains. It sits on the border between Nepal and China. For centuries, people had to work hard just to reach the mountain, never mind climb it.

In 1953, Edmund Hillary and Tenzing Norgay became the first people to climb Mount Everest. Since then, thousands of others have tried to climb it. Many fail. But they still claim that the experience is unique and incredible.

Now some people are saying that Everest is too dangerous for most climbers. The facts back them up. Many Everest climbers die in the attempt. People are also saying that the environment of Everest can't support so many climbers. Climbers use up valuable natural resources, and they leave behind a lot of trash.

1. Why was Everest a tough place to get to?
- ⭘ **A.** It sits on a border.
- ⭘ **B.** It lies deep in the Himalayas.
- ⭘ **C.** Its peak is the highest on Earth.
- ⭘ **D.** People die climbing it.

2. Which of the following is an *opinion*?
- ⭘ **A.** Many Everest climbers die trying to climb the mountain.
- ⭘ **B.** Mount Everest is the highest place on earth.
- ⭘ **C.** Climbing Everest is an incredible experience.
- ⭘ **D.** Everest sits on a border.

3. From this story you can conclude that
- ⭘ **A.** Everest is very difficult to climb.
- ⭘ **B.** Tenzing Norgay died climbing Mount Everest.
- ⭘ **C.** It's easy to collect the trash on Everest.
- ⭘ **D.** Edmund Hillary didn't want others to climb Everest.

VOCABULARY
Which Word Is Missing?

In each of the following paragraphs, a words is missing. First, read each paragraph. Then choose the missing word from the list beneath the paragraph. Fill in the circle next to the word that is missing.

Sample:

Jerome's dad belongs to the neighborhood safety association. Last night, it was his turn to _____ the block. He walked up and down all night, keeping everyone safe.

○ **A.** sweep   ○ **C.** patrol
○ **B.** leave   ○ **D.** study

I. When airplanes were first _____ they were small and relatively slow. However, today's jets can go very fast. Some go faster than the speed of sound!

○ **A.** improved   ○ **C.** searched
○ **B.** repaired   ○ **D.** invented

2. One thing that hasn't changed is the seriousness of a pilot's job. A pilot should never be _____. Doing careless or dangerous things risks lives.

○ **A.** reckless   ○ **C.** energetic
○ **B.** accurate   ○ **D.** strict

3. Passengers are certainly more comfortable than they used to be. Old jet planes were very noisy. People used to wear earplugs to keep out the _____.

○ **A.** filth   ○ **C.** din
○ **B.** music   ○ **D.** moisture

4. Airports have changed, too. Passengers used to walk onto the runway when getting on and off the plane. Now, upon _____, the plane parks at a gate that leads right inside the airport.

○ **A.** transportation   ○ **C.** publication
○ **B.** landscape   ○ **D.** arrival

5. _____ handling has really improved as well. These days people wait a much shorter time to pick up their suitcases after a flight.

○ **A.** Security   ○ **C.** Refund
○ **B.** Disturbance   ○ **D.** Baggage

6. Many people would say that having chocolate cake for _____ is a great treat. They can't think of a better way to end dinner.

○ **A.** lunch   ○ **C.** dessert
○ **B.** delightful   ○ **D.** menu

7. It's rare that people will leave even a _____ of chocolate cake on their plates. They want to eat every bite.

○ **A.** morsel   ○ **C.** mortal
○ **B.** meager   ○ **D.** variety

8. For them, a delicious chocolate cake is absolute _____. Nothing could make it better.

○ **A.** elegant   ○ **C.** keen
○ **B.** perfection   ○ **D.** perilous

9. Chocolate is native to the Americas. Its _____ smell has been making people's mouth's water for a long time.

○ **A.** unpleasant   ○ **C.** amusing
○ **B.** delightful   ○ **D.** entertaining

10. Today, a chocolate _____ can produce many different products. A chocolate factory might make candy bars, cocoa powder, chocolate-chip cookies, and lots of other delicious treats.

○ **A.** gourmet   ○ **C.** manufacturer
○ **B.** compound   ○ **D.** provision

Reading Skills Practice Test 12

READING COMPREHENSION

Read each story. Then fill in the circle that best completes each sentence or answers each question.

When the *Titanic* sank, in 1912, the disaster became a hot topic for the entertainment industry. The first *Titanic* movie opened one month after the disaster. It starred Dorothy Gibson, an actress who had actually survived the disaster. And even 85 years later, another *Titanic* movie was a **blockbuster**, wowing crowds everywhere.

1. This story is mostly about
   - ○ **A.** the sinking of the *Titanic*.
   - ○ **B.** the building of the *Titanic*.
   - ○ **C.** movies about the *Titanic*.
   - ○ **D.** survivors of the *Titanic*.

2. In this story, the word **blockbuster** means
   - ○ **A.** failure.
   - ○ **B.** success.
   - ○ **C.** wreck.
   - ○ **D.** ship.

A. Was your winter weather crazy this year? If so, the culprit may have been El Niño, a weather pattern that happens every three to five years. The trouble starts in the Pacific Ocean when trade winds slow down. With less wind to blow the sun-warmed water away, normal cooling does not take place, and ocean temperatures rise. Warm water creates more moisture in the air, and so more rain falls in some places. This causes more rain to fall in many spots in North and South America. In addition, the changing winds push warm water away from Asia, Africa, and Australia. The resulting droughts that occur on these three continents can cause wildfires.

1. What is the best title for this story?
   - ○ **A.** "More Fish in the Ocean"
   - ○ **B.** "Rain!"
   - ○ **C.** "How El Niño Affects Weather"
   - ○ **D.** "Weather Above the Pacific Ocean"

2. Which part of El Niño happens first?
   - ○ **A.** Wildfires occur.
   - ○ **B.** Ocean temperatures rise.
   - ○ **C.** There is moisture in the air.
   - ○ **D.** Rain hits North and South America.

3. How can El Niño cause fires?
   - ○ **A.** The sun is hotter than usual.
   - ○ **B.** Less rain in some areas causes a drought that can lead to fires.
   - ○ **C.** The ocean water is warmer and can cause fires.
   - ○ **D.** The ocean water disappears.

B.   How would you describe the typical American kid?

If you just watched TV news, you might get the idea that many kids are involved in crime. But that media image is wrong. Only a tiny percentage of kids in this country actually commit crimes. Most American kids are law-abiding citizens.

What's another **misconception**? Some adults think that kids today have too much time on their hands. But many teens will tell you a different story. In addition to school, kids have homework, sports, music lessons, chores, and other activities. These kids are too busy to be bored!

1. What is the best title for this story?
   ○ **A.** "Misconceptions About American Kids"
   ○ **B.** "Violent Crime in America"
   ○ **C.** "Busy, Busy, Busy!"
   ○ **D.** "Kids Around the World"

2. According to the story, which is true?
   ○ **A.** Most kids commit crimes.
   ○ **B.** American kids aren't very busy.
   ○ **C.** Newspapers don't report crime.
   ○ **D.** Few American kids commit crimes.

3. In this story the word **misconception** means
   ○ **A.** information.   ○ **C.** wrong idea.
   ○ **B.** small detail.   ○ **D.** point.

C.   The Philippines is a beautiful country. This nation in southeast Asia is made up of many islands. Its capital, Manila, is located on Luzon, the largest of the islands. In the north of Luzon, rice is grown in paddies. These rice paddies are unique and attract tourists from all over the world.

Other islands in the Philippines attract tourists as well. Palawan, the westernmost island, is popular with snorkelers and divers because it has beautiful coral reefs. Another popular Palawan tourist attraction is the Underground River, which runs through a cave. You can canoe down this river for over half a mile. You'll see enormous caves with one-hundred foot ceilings, and giant stalagmites and stalactites. But this ride is not for the squeamish. All over the cave walls and ceilings, thousands of bats are sleeping— upside down!

1. Where is the Philippines located?
   ○ **A.** Northern Africa
   ○ **B.** Southeast Asia
   ○ **C.** Central Asia
   ○ **D.** Australia

2. From the story, you might conclude that
   ○ **A.** the author doesn't know very much about the Philippines.
   ○ **B.** the author hates the Philippines.
   ○ **C.** coral reefs are under water.
   ○ **D.** the Philippines is a poor country.

3. The main purpose of this story is to
   ○ **A.** inform.   ○ **C.** persuade.
   ○ **B.** entertain.   ○ **D.** amuse.

4. Which of these is an *opinion* about the Philippines?
   ○ **A.** It is made up of many islands.
   ○ **B.** It is a beautiful country.
   ○ **C.** Palawan is its westernmost island.
   ○ **D.** Palawan is popular with snorkelers.

D.   Have you ever heard of "rappelling"? This form of mountaineering involves attaching yourself to a rope and harness and descending a steep slope. Instead of climbing down with your hands and feet, you actually walk down the slope backwards. It's certainly a quick—and scary—way to get down a mountain. Or, in my case, a waterfall!

   The first time I went rappelling was down a mountain waterfall. It was over 70 feet high, and the water rushed over it furiously. My guide clipped me into a harness, attached a safety rope, and sent me over the side of the **torrent** of water. At first, I was terrified and hung on for dear life. But, after a while, I realized that I wouldn't fall, so I relaxed and began to enjoy my descent. After all, few people can say they have walked on a waterfall!

I.   In this story the word **torrent** means
   ○ **A.** large amount.   ○ **C.** rope harness.
   ○ **B.** gentle slope.   ○ **D.** activity.

2.   From this story, you might guess that
   ○ **A.** the narrator hated rappelling.
   ○ **B.** waterfalls have warm water.
   ○ **C.** rappelling is quite easy to do.
   ○ **D.** the author's guide was a rappeller.

3.   This story would probably be found in a
   ○ **A.** sports magazine.
   ○ **B.** poetry book.
   ○ **C.** newspaper.
   ○ **D.** textbook.

4.   The next paragraph might talk about
   ○ **A.** how waterfalls are created.
   ○ **B.** the author's next rappelling experience.
   ○ **C.** water pollution.
   ○ **D.** walking backwards.

E.   Can a sea lion be trained to use a video camera? That's what a scientist, Dr. James Harvey, wanted to find out. He trained two sea lions named Beaver and Sake to use video cameras underwater. With the cameras strapped to their backs, the sea lions filmed gray whales diving off the coast of California. The video helped Harvey learn more about how the whales behave in the deep sea.

   Harvey says humans can't dive deep enough to film the whales. Humans also sometimes scare the whales away. Sea lions are just right for the job because whales are not afraid of them.

   Beaver and Sake practiced swimming near an **artificial** whale. They needed to stay close to the nose of the whale to get the best shots.

I.   In this story, the word **artificial** means
   ○ **A.** fake.   ○ **C.** lively.
   ○ **B.** cute.   ○ **D.** enormous.

2.   The main idea of this story is that
   ○ **A.** sea lions can help scientists study gray whales.
   ○ **B.** sea lions are cute and cuddly.
   ○ **C.** gray whales are interesting animals.
   ○ **D.** sea lions have to practice before using video cameras in the ocean.

3.   Beaver and Sake got ready to study gray whales by
   ○ **A.** playing with them.
   ○ **B.** performing tricks at a theme park.
   ○ **C.** diving as deep as they can.
   ○ **D.** swimming near an artificial whale.

4.   You can guess from the story that
   ○ **A.** people want to learn about whales.
   ○ **B.** sea lions are smarter than whales.
   ○ **C.** people can't dive in the ocean.
   ○ **D.** scientists don't have time to film whales.

VOCABULARY

Synonyms

Read the underlined word in each phrase. Mark the word below it that has the same (or close to the same) meaning.

Sample:

ascend the mountain
- ○ **A.** go up
- ○ **B.** go down
- ○ **C.** view
- ○ **D.** walk

1. downhearted mood
   - ○ **A.** pleasant
   - ○ **B.** sad
   - ○ **C.** light
   - ○ **D.** angry

2. interesting fragrance
   - ○ **A.** scene
   - ○ **B.** race
   - ○ **C.** scent
   - ○ **D.** word

3. loud chortle
   - ○ **A.** laugh
   - ○ **B.** cry
   - ○ **C.** scream
   - ○ **D.** sigh

4. precise directions
   - ○ **A.** long
   - ○ **B.** good
   - ○ **C.** direct
   - ○ **D.** exact

5. luminous star
   - ○ **A.** falling
   - ○ **B.** shooting
   - ○ **C.** big
   - ○ **D.** glowing

6. expand the business
   - ○ **A.** make bigger
   - ○ **B.** ruin
   - ○ **C.** sell
   - ○ **D.** earn

7. blend the ingredients
   - ○ **A.** taste
   - ○ **B.** cook
   - ○ **C.** mix
   - ○ **D.** shake

Antonyms

Read the underlined word in each phrase. Mark the word below it that means the opposite or nearly the opposite.

Sample:

endless story
- ○ **A.** funny
- ○ **B.** serious
- ○ **C.** brief
- ○ **D.** long

1. gigantic skyscraper
   - ○ **A.** huge
   - ○ **B.** new
   - ○ **C.** small
   - ○ **D.** glistening

2. reject the idea
   - ○ **A.** care
   - ○ **B.** accept
   - ○ **C.** outline
   - ○ **D.** share

3. tart lemonade
   - ○ **A.** sweet
   - ○ **B.** cool
   - ○ **C.** yellow
   - ○ **D.** sour

4. limber muscles
   - ○ **A.** stiff
   - ○ **B.** large
   - ○ **C.** relaxed
   - ○ **D.** small

5. murky water
   - ○ **A.** muddy
   - ○ **B.** polluted
   - ○ **C.** clear
   - ○ **D.** flowing

6. confront the group
   - ○ **A.** help
   - ○ **B.** remember
   - ○ **C.** avoid
   - ○ **D.** raise

7. frantic call
   - ○ **A.** energetic
   - ○ **B.** late
   - ○ **C.** annoying
   - ○ **D.** calm

Reading Skills Practice Test 13

READING COMPREHENSION

Read each story. Then fill in the circle that best completes each sentence or answers each question.

Underwater photographer Franklin Viola often dives deep under the ocean surface. But when he comes back up, he must rest for a few minutes at a depth of 15 feet. This allows his body to adjust to changes in water pressure. How does Franklin pass the time? He blows bubbles! Franklin can blow bubbles up to four feet in circumference.

I. Why does Franklin rest for a few minutes when he comes back up?
- ○ **A.** He needs to blow bubbles.
- ○ **B.** He needs to rest because he's tired.
- ○ **C.** He needs time for his body to adjust to changes in water pressure.
- ○ **D.** He needs time to blow big bubbles.

A. A young deer injures a leg. A newborn possum gets separated from its parents. In the wilderness, hurt or lost animals can find themselves in trouble—unless they find Auna Badke first.

Auna, a biologist at Foxwood Wildlife Rehabilitation Center in Bristol, Indiana, is dedicated to helping injured or orphaned wildlife. Even as a young girl, Auna helped dozens of lost or injured animals by feeding them and becoming their adopted mom before returning them to their homes in the woods and wetlands. "We have to respect animals and all living things," says Auna.

Auna had a special skill for feeding animals, especially very young ones. She sat with a baby fawn on her lap and waited patiently until it started nibbling her finger. Then she substituted a bottle filled with a formula made from goat's milk. Sometimes she had to feed a baby deer for a year before it was ready to be on its own.

I. From this story, you can conclude that
- ○ **A.** Auna really loves animals.
- ○ **B.** Auna doesn't care about animals.
- ○ **C.** animals never need human help.
- ○ **D.** it's easy to feed baby animals.

2. What is the best title for this story?
- ○ **A.** "A Friend to Animals"
- ○ **B.** "Baby Animals"
- ○ **C.** "How to Feed a Baby Deer"
- ○ **D.** "How Animals Get Hurt"

3. The main purpose of this article is to
- ○ **A.** persuade you to help animals in trouble.
- ○ **B.** inform you about Auna and what she has done.
- ○ **C.** warn you to avoid injured animals.
- ○ **D.** amuse you with a cute animal story.

B. In New York State, some pesky critters may be playing a deadly trick on a Halloween treat. Scientists think that microbes, or bugs so small that they can't be seen without a microscope, are to blame for a strange disease cropping up in some pumpkin patches.

The disease clogs tiny vessels, or tubes, inside the pumpkins. These tubes carry water and nutrients. When the vessels are blocked, pumpkins can't get the **nourishment** they need. So they starve. Infected pumpkins lose their bright-orange color and eventually rot.

The mysterious disease has also been spotted in New York squash and cucumbers. But that doesn't mean people should start worrying about a vegetable shortage. The sick veggies are only a small percentage of the pumpkin, squash, and cucumber crops. So those who were secretly hoping for a few vegetable-free meals better get ready for second helpings instead.

l. In this article, the word **nourishment** means
○ **A.** bugs.
○ **B.** care.
○ **C.** sunlight.
○ **D.** food and water.

2. How does the disease kill pumpkins?
○ **A.** It clogs vessels inside the pumpkins.
○ **B.** It clogs the pumpkin plants' roots.
○ **C.** It makes the pumpkins lose their orange color.
○ **D.** It makes the pumpkins stop growing.

3. What do scientists think is causing the pumpkin disease?
○ **A.** humans
○ **B.** bad weather
○ **C.** microbes
○ **D.** insects

C. It's July and you have to mow the lawn. You grab your robot grass cutter and toss it in the backyard. Minutes later, the frisbee-shaped robot is nibbling away at the grass, and you're headed for the beach.

Yes, mowing the lawn has become that simple, says Mark W. Tilden, a scientist who studies robots. Tilden shares his Los Alamos, New Mexico, home with more than 50 robots. His robotic roommates range from credit-card-sized floor cleaners to creatures that report on break-ins. Others wash windows, kill flies, and yes, cut the grass.

Tilden's robots don't rely on humans to power them. Instead, they draw energy from the sun, lamps, and televisions. Tilden constructs his robots from pieces of broken VCRs, computers, calculators, CD players, TVs, and toys—anything he can find. "All the parts you need to build a robot are sitting in the bottom of your junk drawer," he says. Whoever thought making robots could be that easy!

l. Tilden's robots draw energy from
○ **A.** televisions.
○ **B.** computers.
○ **C.** VCRs.
○ **D.** CD players.

2. Which of these is an *opinion*?
○ **A.** Others wash windows, kill flies, and cut the grass.
○ **B.** Robots can cut grass.
○ **C.** Making robots is easy!
○ **D.** Tilden shares his New Mexico home with more than 50 robots.

3. You can guess from this story that
○ **A.** Tilden thinks robots are boring.
○ **B.** Tilden thinks robots are really cool.
○ **C.** Robots wouldn't be very good at mowing the lawn.
○ **D.** Robots require lots of unique parts.

D. Last year, one of Michaela Clovis's classmates insulted her hair. "She said it doesn't look right and doesn't match my skin," said Michaela, a New Jersey student. Michaela is Irish, German, Native American, and African American. She has fair skin and strawberry-blonde hair, but she is not white.

Soon, a few classmates joined the teasing. One said she couldn't be black and white at the same time. Michaela said she felt "small and alone." But she stopped the taunting without anger or frustration. Here's how she did it.

First, Michaela talked to her parents. Her mother, Donna, told Michaela's teacher and also suggested that Michaela not face the insults alone. Next, Donna told Michaela about the different people in her family, and their love for each other. She taught her that people of all races are beautiful.

That helped Michaela grow more **confident**. The next time she was teased, Michaela said, "I'm mixed, and I'm proud of it." She stuck to that answer until the teasing finally ended.

I. What did Michaela do first to stop the taunting?
○ **A.** She told her teacher.
○ **B.** She told her parents.
○ **C.** She hit the taunters.
○ **D.** She stood her ground until they stopped.

2. In this story, the word **confident** means
○ **A.** nervous and shy.
○ **B.** happy and smiling.
○ **C.** older and wiser.
○ **D.** sure and strong.

3. From this story, you can conclude that
○ **A.** it's possible to end a bad situation without anger or frustration.
○ **B.** people who are teased deserve what they get.
○ **C.** adults can't really help a bad situation.
○ **D.** the best way to end a bad situation is by becoming friends with those who are bothering you.

E. Since they first rescued Missy from an animal shelter when she was just 4 months old, Missy's owners knew they had a perfect dog. So they wanted another one just like her!

The couple hired a team of scientists to clone, or make a copy of, Missy. If they had been successful, Missy's owners would have had the world's first cloned pet.

Missy's owners insisted that Missy had the perfect bark and growl. But the doctor in charge of the "Missyplicity" project warned that Missy's clone might be very different from Missy herself. "You're not getting your old pet back," the doctor said. "You're getting a new pet that has the same genes as the old one."

Genes determine how living things grow. But genes are only half of the story. The environment is also very important. So living conditions could make Missy's clone different from Missy.

Missy died in 2002 before the cloning succeeded. But scientists did succeed in cloning a dog in 2005.

I. What could make Missy's clone different from Missy?
○ **A.** her genes   ○ **C.** her tail
○ **B.** her environment   ○ **D.** her bark

2. What's the best title for this story?
○ **A.** "Dogs, Dogs, Dogs"
○ **B.** "How Our Genes Work"
○ **C.** "Cloning Missy"
○ **D.** "Why Mutts Make the Best Dogs"

VOCABULARY

Synonyms

Read the underlined word in each phrase. Mark the word below it that has the same (or close to the same) meaning.

Sample:

<u>amble</u> along
- ○ **A.** run
- ○ **C.** jog
- ○ **B.** stroll
- ○ **D.** skip

---

1. <u>gnaw</u> a bone
   - ○ **A.** chew
   - ○ **C.** spit out
   - ○ **B.** swallow
   - ○ **D.** lick

2. <u>erect</u> posture
   - ○ **A.** slumped
   - ○ **C.** bent
   - ○ **B.** upright
   - ○ **D.** slouching

3. <u>former</u> president
   - ○ **A.** current
   - ○ **C.** next
   - ○ **B.** previous
   - ○ **D.** future

4. <u>vacant</u> house
   - ○ **A.** occupied
   - ○ **C.** old
   - ○ **B.** empty
   - ○ **D.** big

5. <u>reveal</u> the truth
   - ○ **A.** show
   - ○ **C.** fight
   - ○ **B.** hide
   - ○ **D.** embrace

6. <u>drastic</u> measure
   - ○ **A.** extreme
   - ○ **C.** effective
   - ○ **B.** ineffective
   - ○ **D.** costly

7. <u>sensitive</u> child
   - ○ **A.** timid
   - ○ **C.** tough
   - ○ **B.** easily hurt
   - ○ **D.** quiet

Antonyms

Read the underlined word in each phrase. Mark the word below it that means the opposite or nearly the opposite.

Sample:

<u>elegant</u> clothes
- ○ **A.** casual
- ○ **C.** new
- ○ **B.** formal
- ○ **D.** old

---

1. <u>pester</u> someone
   - ○ **A.** meet
   - ○ **C.** bother
   - ○ **B.** help
   - ○ **D.** ignore

2. <u>lousy</u> idea
   - ○ **A.** great
   - ○ **C.** creative
   - ○ **B.** terrible
   - ○ **D.** silly

3. <u>vivid</u> colors
   - ○ **A.** dull
   - ○ **C.** pastel
   - ○ **B.** bright
   - ○ **D.** loud

4. <u>suitable</u> outfit
   - ○ **A.** inappropriate
   - ○ **C.** ugly
   - ○ **B.** perfect
   - ○ **D.** coordinated

5. <u>deny</u> all charges
   - ○ **A.** admit
   - ○ **C.** write
   - ○ **B.** laugh
   - ○ **D.** spend

6. <u>flammable</u> cloth
   - ○ **A.** aflame
   - ○ **C.** fireproof
   - ○ **B.** flimsy
   - ○ **D.** stiff

7. <u>homely</u> appearance
   - ○ **A.** plain
   - ○ **C.** ugly
   - ○ **B.** attractive
   - ○ **D.** unattractive

Reading Skills Practice Test 14

READING COMPREHENSION

Read each story. Then fill in the circle that best completes each sentence or answers each question.

SAMPLE

Despite their danger to humans, rattlesnakes rarely kill each other. When two rattlers fight, they never deliver a deadly bite. Instead, they lift their heads and push each other. The snake that gets pushed to the ground slinks away. The instinct not to kill each other helps keep the species alive.

1. What is the best title for this story?
   ○ A. "Endangered Snakes"
   ○ B. "Snakes of the World"
   ○ C. "How Rattlesnakes Fight"
   ○ D. "Rattlesnake Bites"

2. After a fight, a losing rattlesnake
   ○ A. bites the winner.
   ○ B. slinks away.
   ○ C. lifts its head.
   ○ D. dies.

A. The Maya were an ancient Central American people who developed a writing system. To write, they used picture symbols called hieroglyphs. They drew or carved the hieroglyphs on pottery, walls, and stone sculptures. Scholars who have learned to decipher Mayan hieroglyphs believe priests and nobles were the only people who could read this writing.

1. Hieroglyphs are
   ○ A. picture symbols.
   ○ B. ornaments.
   ○ C. pottery.
   ○ D. letters.

2. You can guess from the story that
   ○ A. the Maya were smarter than other people.
   ○ B. some Mayan hieroglyphs have been discovered.
   ○ C. hieroglyphs are a lot like our own form of writing.
   ○ D. hieroglyphs are colorful.

B. Do you know how to make rice? First, measure out the exact amount of rice you need. Then rinse the rice several times in cold water. Put it in a pot with exactly twice as much water as rice. Place the pot over medium heat and bring it to a boil. When it comes to a boil cover the pot tightly with a lid and turn the heat down very low. Let it cook for exactly 17 minutes. Don't peek! Then turn off the heat and let the pot of rice stand for another 5 minutes. Finally fluff it with a fork.

1. What is the best title for this story?
   - ○ **A.** "How to Cook Rice"
   - ○ **B.** "Using the Stove"
   - ○ **C.** "How to Serve Rice"
   - ○ **D.** "Slow Cooking"

2. Right after you cover the pot with a lid, you should
   - ○ **A.** rinse the rice.
   - ○ **B.** turn down the heat.
   - ○ **C.** add water.
   - ○ **D.** fluff the rice with a fork.

3. The purpose of this story is to
   - ○ **A.** inform.
   - ○ **B.** persuade.
   - ○ **C.** entertain.
   - ○ **D.** inspire.

C. Scientists say houseplants do more than decorate homes and offices. They can also improve the quality of the air we breathe. Buildings today are often airtight and have plenty of insulation. This makes them energy-efficient, but it also makes it hard for fresh air to enter.

Many houseplants can "clean" the stale air trapped inside buildings. Plant leaves take in carbon dioxide gas from the air. In return, they give out clean oxygen. Plants also take other dangerous gases from the air. For instance, a type of daisy takes in benzene, a chemical found in gasoline. Spider plants take in carbon monoxide. So why not keep a lot of houseplants around? They just might help you breathe easier.

1. Spider plants take in
   - ○ **A.** oxygen.
   - ○ **B.** insulation.
   - ○ **C.** benzene.
   - ○ **D.** carbon monoxide.

2. Why can't fresh air enter many newer buildings?
   - ○ **A.** They do not have enough spider plants.
   - ○ **B.** They are airtight and have a lot of insulation.
   - ○ **C.** They are too full of oxygen.
   - ○ **D.** They have too many people.

3. Which of these is an *opinion* about plants?
   - ○ **A.** They take in gas.
   - ○ **B.** They look beautiful.
   - ○ **C.** They give out oxygen.
   - ○ **D.** They are found in some offices.

D.   Most parts of your body have a job to do. Not the appendix! The appendix is a three-inch-long, worm-shaped part of the intestines. While the appendix no longer appears to have a **function**, scientists think it was once an important part of the human digestive system. Some animals, like rabbits, still need an appendix. The organ helps them digest tough plant food.

Although the appendix may not do humans any good, it can do a lot of harm. If a person's appendix becomes infected by bacteria, he or she can suffer an attack of appendicitis. The symptoms include pain, nausea, and fever. If the appendix bursts, the infection can spread throughout the body. To prevent that from happening, a doctor will usually remove an infected appendix.

I. The main idea of this story is that
   ○ **A.** humans and rabbits both have an appendix.
   ○ **B.** an appendix can burst.
   ○ **C.** the human appendix is not useful, but it is dangerous when infected.
   ○ **D.** every organ has a job.

2. In this story the word **function** means
   ○ **A.** organ.
   ○ **B.** life.
   ○ **C.** job.
   ○ **D.** cause.

3. You can guess from this story that
   ○ **A.** a person can live without an appendix.
   ○ **B.** a rabbit can live without an appendix.
   ○ **C.** the appendix is important.
   ○ **D.** humans never eat plants.

E.   Bolivia is a South American country that borders Peru, Chile, Argentina, Brazil, and Paraguay. It has a variety of landscapes. The north of Bolivia is mainly tropical rain forest. The Amazon River snakes through the steamy forest. Since there aren't many roads, people often travel through this area on riverboats. The forest is home to many kinds of wildlife, including toucans, jaguars, and capybaras, the world's largest rodents.

Bolivia's capital, La Paz, is in the snow-capped Andes mountains. At more than 12,000 feet, it is the highest capital in the world! Unlike the rainy, humid rain forest, this mountain area is extremely **arid**.

I. In this story, the word **arid** means
   ○ **A.** wet.
   ○ **B.** hot.
   ○ **C.** dry.
   ○ **D.** cool.

2. Bolivia's capital is special because
   ○ **A.** it's in the rain forest.
   ○ **B.** it's in the Andes.
   ○ **C.** it has capybaras.
   ○ **D.** it's the highest capital in the world.

3. This story would probably go on to talk about
   ○ **A.** mountains.
   ○ **B.** other places in South America.
   ○ **C.** tropical birds.
   ○ **D.** North America.

VOCABULARY

Synonyms

Read the underlined word in each phrase. Mark the word below it that has the same (or close to the same) meaning.

Sample:

reluctant to go
- ○ **A.** eager
- ○ **B.** hesitant
- ○ **C.** late
- ○ **D.** surprised

1. gape at
   - ○ **A.** sneer
   - ○ **B.** squint
   - ○ **C.** smile
   - ○ **D.** stare

2. minor problems
   - ○ **A.** small
   - ○ **B.** large
   - ○ **C.** difficult
   - ○ **D.** easy

3. with liberty
   - ○ **A.** triumph
   - ○ **B.** unwilling
   - ○ **C.** freedom
   - ○ **D.** surprise

4. frail child
   - ○ **A.** unfriendly
   - ○ **B.** delicate
   - ○ **C.** strong
   - ○ **D.** feverish

5. perilous journey
   - ○ **A.** long
   - ○ **B.** uncomfortable
   - ○ **C.** interesting
   - ○ **D.** dangerous

6. sole survivor
   - ○ **A.** first
   - ○ **B.** only
   - ○ **C.** last
   - ○ **D.** oldest

7. feeling uneasy
   - ○ **A.** unfit
   - ○ **B.** difficult
   - ○ **C.** disappointed
   - ○ **D.** uncomfortable

Antonyms

Read the underlined word in each phrase. Mark the word below it that means the opposite or nearly the opposite.

Sample:

spectacular event
- ○ **A.** amazing
- ○ **B.** joyful
- ○ **C.** tragic
- ○ **D.** ordinary

1. driving recklessly
   - ○ **A.** cautiously
   - ○ **B.** wildly
   - ○ **C.** slowly
   - ○ **D.** carelessly

2. inferior brand
   - ○ **A.** exterior
   - ○ **B.** popular
   - ○ **C.** superior
   - ○ **D.** expensive

3. prolong the class
   - ○ **A.** lengthen
   - ○ **B.** shorten
   - ○ **C.** end
   - ○ **D.** begin

4. feel panic
   - ○ **A.** calm
   - ○ **B.** upset
   - ○ **C.** disgust
   - ○ **D.** content

5. amateur athlete
   - ○ **A.** gifted
   - ○ **B.** competitive
   - ○ **C.** professional
   - ○ **D.** untalented

6. solemn occasion
   - ○ **A.** frequent
   - ○ **B.** rare
   - ○ **C.** sorry
   - ○ **D.** cheerful

7. spare part
   - ○ **A.** needed
   - ○ **B.** extra
   - ○ **C.** loose
   - ○ **D.** costly

Reading Skills Practice Test 15

READING COMPREHENSION

Read each story. Then fill in the circle that best completes each sentence or answers each question.

At age 28, Los Angeles Lakers basketball star Shaquille "Shaq" O'Neal slam-dunked his education and scored. How? He graduated from Louisiana State University. The 7-foot, 1-inch player had dropped out of college to play basketball. At the time, he promised his mom that he would finish college. He kept his word, and returned eight years later.

I. What did Shaq promise his mom?
- ○ **A.** That he would finish college.
- ○ **B.** That he would return to college when he was 28.
- ○ **C.** That he would become a great basketball player.
- ○ **D.** That he would join the Lakers.

2. How many years after dropping out of college did Shaq return?
- ○ **A.** 28
- ○ **B.** 7
- ○ **C.** 1
- ○ **D.** 8

A. Cuddles, a tiny pony, isn't horsing around. She is training to be the world's first guide horse for blind people. Cuddles and some of her fellow miniature horses are being trained like Seeing Eye dogs.

"Guide horses are not meant to compete with Seeing Eye dogs, but are meant to give blind people more **options**," says Don Burleson, who in 1999 started the non-profit Guide Horse Foundation with his wife, Janet.

Burleson says mini-horses will make good guides for blind people. The horses—which grow no taller than 34 inches at the shoulder and weigh between 150 and 250 pounds—have excellent vision, a good memory, and live 30 to 40 years. That's at least three times longer than a guide dog, whose life span averages 10 years.

The long life span is what convinced Dan Shaw to sign up to get the first guide horse. "Instead of going through three or four guide dogs in my lifetime, I'll get to stick with one animal," he says.

I. In this passage, the word **options** means
- ○ **A.** animals
- ○ **B.** help
- ○ **C.** choices
- ○ **D.** friends

2. You can conclude that Burleson thinks mini-horses make good guides for blind people because
- ○ **A.** they have excellent vision, a good memory, and they live longer than guide dogs.
- ○ **B.** they are smarter than guide dogs.
- ○ **C.** they never bite people.
- ○ **D.** they can sleep indoors.

3. What convinced Dan Shaw to get the first guide horse?
- ○ **A.** He likes horses better than dogs.
- ○ **B.** He likes the fact that they weigh between 150 and 250 pounds.
- ○ **C.** He will be able to stick with one animal for many years.
- ○ **D.** He used to ride horses when he was younger.

B.   Every summer, Alisia Orosco, went in and out of the hospital. But Alisia wasn't sick. While a student at Black Middle School in Abilene, Texas, Alisia delivered stuffed animals to young patients who needed a friend.

"My baby brother used to have to be in the hospital all the time, but he was happy because he had Winnie the Pooh," said Alisia. She realized other kids in the hospital could use some fuzzy friends, too.

In 1996, Alisia and her older brother saved their allowances to buy 15 stuffed animals. They gave them to patients at nearby hospitals. The response was so good, Alisia continued saving. Eventually she visited three hospitals regularly with bags of donated toys. "I hope to help as many kids as I can," Alisia said. "It makes me happy to make them smile."

I.   How did Alisia say she felt when she helped people?
○ **A.** proud   ○ **B.** sad
○ **C.** tired   ○ **D.** happy

2.   What made Alisia first realize that kids in hospitals might like getting stuffed animals?
○ **A.** She had to stay in the hospital herself.
○ **B.** She saw that her baby brother liked having a stuffed Winnie the Pooh when he was in the hospital.
○ **C.** Her older brother told her to donate her stuffed animals.
○ **D.** She visited three hospitals regularly with bags of toys.

3.   What did Alisia and her older brother do in 1996?
○ **A.** saved their allowances to buy 15 stuffed animals for patients at nearby hospitals
○ **B.** volunteered at a local hospital
○ **C.** went to summer camp
○ **D.** had an argument about whose job it was to bring stuffed animals to the hospital

---

C.   The world's tigers are roaring back to life. Tiger experts had once predicted the big cats would be nearly **extinct** by the year 2000. But in a recent report from the National Tiger Conservation Authority, conservationists, or people who save wildlife, agreed that the population of the largest member of the cat family appears to be on the rise.

Most tigers live in Asian nations, including Sumatra, Burma, India, and Thailand. In these countries, tigers have faced serious threats to their survival. Poachers, or people who kill wild animals and sell the body parts, hunted tigers for profit. Historically, many people in China have used tiger bones to make medicine for muscular aches and pains.

Now, many Asian countries are arresting poachers. And many Chinese people are trying to use alternatives to tiger bones for their medicines.

In the early 1970s, 50,000 to 70,000 tigers lived in Asia. Today, only a few thousand survive in the wild. But instead of falling even lower, the number is on the rise once again. In India, for example, the numbers have increased nearly 60% since 2008.

Now that's something to roar about!

I.   Which is a *fact*?
○ **A.** Tigers belong in the zoo.
○ **B.** Most tigers live in Asian nations.
○ **C.** Most tigers are scary.
○ **D.** It's important to help save tigers.

2.   How is the number of tigers in Asia today different from the number of tigers there in the 1970s?
○ **A.** There are fewer tigers in Asia today.
○ **B.** There are more tigers in Asia today.
○ **C.** There are the same number of tigers in Asia today.
○ **D.** There are no tigers in Asia today.

3.   In this article, the word **extinct** means
○ **A.** smelly   ○ **C.** rising
○ **B.** alive   ○ **D.** dead

D.   Kellie Vaughn was a poet but didn't know it—at least not until she was 12. Desperate for a Father's Day gift, she **penned** her first poem in honor of her dad.

"Before then, I hated to write anything," says the Huntsville, Alabama, native. "Poetry has taught me about myself and the world around me."

Now, Kellie is a prize-winning poet. She also started a poetry website just for children. Many kids send in poems about friendship, family, or school. Some of the poems rhyme, and some do not. Kellie believes any subject or form is fine. "It's about what flows from your mind," she says.

1.   In this story, the word **penned** means
   ○ **A.** bought
   ○ **B.** drew
   ○ **C.** read
   ○ **D.** wrote

2.   Which is an *opinion*?
   ○ **A.** Kellie Vaughn started a website for kids' poetry.
   ○ **B.** Kellie has won prizes for her own poetry.
   ○ **C.** It is hard to write poems.
   ○ **D.** Poems do not all rhyme.

3.   According to Kellie, poems should be about
   ○ **A.** rainbows and flowers.
   ○ **B.** what flows from your mind.
   ○ **C.** your father or mother.
   ○ **D.** the President of the United States.

E.   Cigarettes kill more than 400,000 Americans each year—more deaths than from alcohol, car accidents, murders, drugs, and fires combined. Every day, 3,000 more kids start smoking. One out of every three young smokers will eventually die from diseases caused by tobacco use.

But if tobacco is so risky, why would anyone smoke?

"A lot of kids are not aware of the dangers of tobacco," said Sarah Schulman of Austin, Texas. As a teenager, Sarah was a youth advocate for the Campaign for Tobacco-Free Kids, a national anti-smoking group. She spoke with kids and adults around the country about the **hazards** of smoking.

According to Sarah, she would often hear from peers who said, "At least I'm not using hard drugs." But tobacco is addictive, Sarah would tell them. "It's a potent drug that kills."

1.   About how many Americans are killed by cigarettes each year?
   ○ **A.** 3,000
   ○ **B.** 14
   ○ **C.** 400,000
   ○ **D.** 700,000

2.   In this article, the word **hazards** means
   ○ **A.** dangers.
   ○ **B.** difficulties.
   ○ **C.** benefits.
   ○ **D.** parts.

3.   Sarah Schulman says that one reason kids smoke is:
   ○ **A.** they are trying to look cool.
   ○ **B.** they want to use hard drugs.
   ○ **C.** they have older brothers or sisters who smoke.
   ○ **D.** they are not aware of the dangers of tobacco.

VOCABULARY

Synonyms

Read the underlined word in each phrase. Mark the word below it that has the same (or close to the same) meaning.

Sample:

departing flight
- ○ **A.** long
- ○ **B.** flying
- ○ **C.** breaking
- ○ **D.** leaving

1. absurd idea
   - ○ **A.** good
   - ○ **B.** ridiculous
   - ○ **C.** interesting
   - ○ **D.** quick

2. tranquil seas
   - ○ **A.** wavy
   - ○ **B.** wet
   - ○ **C.** calm
   - ○ **D.** cold

3. menacing dog
   - ○ **A.** threatening
   - ○ **B.** furry
   - ○ **C.** friendly
   - ○ **D.** large

4. diminish in number
   - ○ **A.** rise
   - ○ **B.** list
   - ○ **C.** count
   - ○ **D.** lessen

5. at dusk
   - ○ **A.** evening
   - ○ **B.** midnight
   - ○ **C.** morning
   - ○ **D.** noon

6. demand an answer
   - ○ **A.** desire
   - ○ **B.** refuse
   - ○ **C.** order
   - ○ **D.** offer

7. eerie noise
   - ○ **A.** loud
   - ○ **B.** quiet
   - ○ **C.** creepy
   - ○ **D.** cheerful

Antonyms

Read the underlined word in each phrase. Mark the word below it that means the opposite or nearly the opposite.

Sample:

dim room
- ○ **A.** dark
- ○ **B.** thick
- ○ **C.** soft
- ○ **D.** bright

1. purchase clothing
   - ○ **A.** shop
   - ○ **B.** carry
   - ○ **C.** take
   - ○ **D.** sell

2. acting ungrateful
   - ○ **A.** thankful
   - ○ **B.** poor
   - ○ **C.** rich
   - ○ **D.** spoiled

3. tardy arrival
   - ○ **A.** skinny
   - ○ **B.** kind
   - ○ **C.** early
   - ○ **D.** late

4. base of the building
   - ○ **A.** ball
   - ○ **B.** top
   - ○ **C.** bat
   - ○ **D.** bottom

5. stop the racket
   - ○ **A.** tennis
   - ○ **B.** cold
   - ○ **C.** silence
   - ○ **D.** din

6. modest improvement
   - ○ **A.** small
   - ○ **B.** big
   - ○ **C.** false
   - ○ **D.** temporary

7. unjust treatment
   - ○ **A.** unfair
   - ○ **B.** fair
   - ○ **C.** unkind
   - ○ **D.** lenient

Answer Key

TEST 1
Sample: 1.A 2.C

Passage A
1.C 2.A 3.C

Passage B
1.B 2.D 3.D

Passage C
1.A 2.D 3.A 4.C

Passage D
1.C 2.B 3.D 4.A

Passage E
1.A 2.B 3.D 4.A

Vocabulary
Which Word Is Missing?
Sample: B
1.D 2.C 3.B 4.A
5.C 6.B

TEST 2
Sample: 1.C 2.B

Passage A
1.B 2.B 3.C

Passage B
1.A 2.D 3.A

Passage C
1.A 2.B

Passage D
1.D 2.B 3.A

Passage E
1.D 2.A 3.C 4.A

Vocabulary
Synonyms
Sample: C
1.A 2.C 3.B 4.A
5.B 6.A 7.B
Antonyms
Sample: B
1.B 2.B 3.D 4.A
5.D 6.C 7.C

TEST 3
Sample: B

Passage A
1.A 2.D 3.B

Passage B
1.B 2.B 3.A

Passage C
1.B 2.D 3.C

Passage D
1.A 2.B 3.D

Passage E
1.A 2.B 3.C

Vocabulary
Synonyms
Sample: B
1.A 2.C 3.B 4.D
5.A 6.B 7.B
Antonyms
Sample: C
1.A 2.D 3.D 4.A
5.C 6.D 7.D

TEST 4
Sample: 1.D 2.B

Passage A
1.B 2.A 3.B

Passage B
1.C 2.B 3.B

Passage C
1.D 2.B 3.B

Passage D
1.A 2.C 3.D 4.D

Passage E
1.A 2. C 3.C

Vocabulary
Synonyms
Sample: D
1.B 2.C 3.A 4.C
5.D 6.C 7.C

Antonyms
Sample: B
1.A 2.B 3.D 4.C
5.A 6.B 7.C

TEST 5
Sample: 1.B 2.C

Passage A
1.D 2.A 3.C

Passage B
1.A 2.B 3.A

Passage C
1.B 2.D

Passage D
1.A 2.D 3.C

Passage E
1.A 2.D 3.C

Passage F.
1.A 2.D 3.B 4.D

Study Skills
Reading a Line Graph
1.C 2.A 3.B 4.D

Reading an Index
1.B 2.A 3.A 4.D

TEST 6
Sample: 1.B 2.A

Passage A
1.D 2.B 3.B

Passage B
1.A 2.D

Passage C
1.C 2.B 3.C

Passage D
1.A 2.C 3.A

Passage E
1.C 2.D 3.C

Vocabulary
Synonyms
Sample: B
1.C 2.A 3.B 4.C
5.A 6.A 7.C
Antonyms
Sample: B
1.A 2.D 3.A 4.B
5.D 6.D 7.B

TEST 7
Sample: 1.A 2.C

Passage A
1.D 2.A 3.C

Passage B
1.A 2.C 3.D

Passage C
1.C 2.B 3.A

Passage D
1.C 2.D 3.A

Passage E
1.B 2.D 3.A

Vocabulary
Synonyms
Sample: A
1.C 2.B 3.C 4.C
5.A 6.B 7.A
Antonyms
Sample: B
1.C 2.A 3.A 4.B
5.D 6.A 7.D

TEST 8
Sample: 1.C 2.D

Passage A
1.B 2.C 3.A

Passage B
1.B 2.D 3.A

Passage C
1.C 2.A 3.B

Passage D
1.D 2.D 3.B

Passage E
1.A 2.C 3.B

Vocabulary
Which Word Is Missing?
Sample: C
1.D 2.A 3.B 4.D
5.A 6.C 7.A 8.D
9.B 10.B

TEST 9
Sample: 1.B 2.A

Passage A
1.D 2.D

Passage B
1.B 2.B 3.C

Passage C
1.C 2.A 3.B 4.D

Passage D
1.A 2.D 3.A

Passage E
1.C 2.B 3.A

Vocabulary
Synonyms
Sample: A
1.D 2.C 3.B 4.D
5.A 6.A 7.B
Antonyms
Sample: D
1.D 2.B 3.D 4.B
5.A 6.C 7.B

TEST 10
Sample: 1.B 2.C

Passage A
1.C 2.B

Passage B
1.A 2.D 3.B

Passage C
1.C 2.D 3.B

Passage D
1.D 2.C 3.B

Passage E
1.B 2.A 3.C

Vocabulary
Synonyms
Sample: D
1.B 2.B 3.B 4.B
5.D 6.A 7.B
Antonyms
Sample: A
1.D 2.D 3.D 4.A
5.D 6.D 7.C

TEST 11
Sample: 1.B 2.D

Passage A
1.A 2.C 3.B

Passage B
1.D 2.C 3.A

Passage C
1.A 2.C 3.B

Passage D
1.C 2.B 3.B 4.D

Passage E
1.B 2.C 3.A

Vocabulary
Sample: C
1.D 2.A 3.C 4.D
5.D 6.C 7.A 8.B
9.B 10.C

TEST 12
Sample: 1.C 2.B

Passage A
1.C 2.B 3.B

Passage B
1.A 2.D 3.C

Passage C
1.B 2.C 3.A 4.B

Passage D
1.A 2.D 3.A 4.B

Passage E
1.A 2.A 3.D 4.A

Vocabulary
Synonyms
Sample: A
1.B 2.C 3.A 4.D
5.D 6.A 7.C
Antonyms
Sample: C
1.C 2.B 3.A 4.A
5.C 6.C 7.D

TEST 13
Sample: 1.C

Passage A
1.A 2.A 3.B

Passage B
1.D 2.A 3.C

Passage C
1.A 2.C 3.B

Passage D
1.B 2.D 3.A

Passage E
1.B 2.C

Vocabulary
Synonyms
Sample: B
1.A 2.B 3.B 4.B
5.A 6.A 7.B
Antonyms
Sample: A
1.D 2.A 3.A 4.A
5.A 6.C 7.B

TEST 14
Sample: 1.C 2.B

Passage A
1.A 2.B

Passage B
1.A 2.B 3.A

Passage C
1.D 2.B 3.B

Passage D
1.C 2.C 3.A

Passage E
1.C 2.D 3.B

Vocabulary
Synonyms
Sample: B
1.D 2.A 3.C 4.B
5.D 6.B 7.D
Antonyms
Sample: D
1.A 2.C 3.B 4.A
5.C 6.D 7.A

TEST 15
Sample: 1.A 2.D

Passage A
1.C 2.A 3.C

Passage B
1.D 2.B 3.A

Passage C
1.B 2.A 3.D

Passage D
1.D 2.C 3.B

Passage E
1.C 2.A 3.D

Vocabulary
Synonyms
Sample: D
1.B 2.C 3.A 4.D
5.A 6.C 7.C
Antonyms
Sample: D
1.D 2.A 3.C 4.B
5.C 6.B 7.B